HAUNTED BUFFALO

HAUNTED BUFFALO

GHOSTS IN THE QUEEN CITY

DWAYNE CLAUD and CASSIDY O'CONNOR
FOREWORD BY RICHARD J. KIMMEL

Haunted America

Published by Haunted America

A Division of The History Press

Charleston, SC 29403

www.historypress.net

All photographs by the authors unless otherwise noted.

First published 2009

Second printing 2010

Manufactured in the United States

ISBN 978.1.59629.775.3

Library of Congress Cataloging-in-Publication Data
Claud, Dwayne.
Haunted Buffalo : ghosts of the Queen City / Dwayne Claud and Cassiday
O'Connor.
p. cm.
Includes bibliographical references and index.
ISBN 978-1-59629-775-3 (alk. paper)
1. Ghosts--New York (State)--Buffalo. 2. Haunted places--New York (State)--
Buffalo. I. O'Connor, Cassiday. II. Title.
BF1472.U6C585 2009
133.109747'97--dc22
2009030604

Book dedications are often made to individuals or organizations that have lended the most assistance in the work's development. For each author, the word dedication takes on its own personal meaning. As an author, Dwayne feels that the strongest inspiration comes from those closest to you. It is for that reason that he would like to dedicate this book to his son Jesse. Jesse is a wonderful twelve-year-old child who sees the world every day with excitement and anticipation. He knows no limitations, taking joy in the smallest of things and finding the amazement in each. Dwayne feels that writing this book and others similar to it has allowed him to catch just a small glimpse of what Jesse's world is like.

People often feel that history is found in books, but Cassidy disagrees. Her stepmother, Wendy O'Connor, allowed her to see history close up even as a small child. Cassidy has memories of crawling through historic grain elevators along the Buffalo waterfront as a child as her stepmother fought for their preservation. It is then that Cassidy learned to appreciate the importance of the preservation of our heritage. Cassidy thanks Wendy O'Connor for the passion she now holds for preserving even the smallest bit of history and for all the wonderful knowledge and love that she was able to share regarding the history of Buffalo for this book.

CONTENTS

FOREWORD

Dwayne Claud is a prolific writer and author of several books, and, without a doubt, this work ranks with the best. Cassidy O'Connor's talent for digging up historical background has added a unique flair to this book, merging the ghostly tales of the region with historical accuracy, in some cases proving, while in others disproving, some reported paranormal phenomenon. *Haunted Buffalo* presents one with the feeling of experiencing the paranormal activity along with the authors, leaving little doubt in the mind of the reader that Buffalo is definitely haunted.

From the history of Buffalo to a crash course in ghost hunting and everything in between, *Haunted Buffalo* presents a completely unique perspective, one that will keep the reader interested from beginning to end. Even if you have never had an interest in the paranormal, you can consider this an excellent general field guide to haunted places in Buffalo.

What impressed me most about *Haunted Buffalo* is that, in each chapter, Dwayne and Cassidy enlighten the reader as to what you can expect at each location. I am certain that once you finish reading, you will be anxious to seek out the haunts and experience them for yourselves.

Thank you, Dwayne and Cassidy, for presenting *Haunted Buffalo* in the manner in which you chose to do and, speaking the vernacular of the paranormal, may the spirits of Buffalo be with you and all the readers of this fine work.

Richard J. Kimmel
Author of *WWII Ghosts—Artifacts Can Talk*

INTRODUCTION

BUFFALO, NEW YORK—A BRIEF HISTORY

The splendor of the great city of Buffalo began over two hundred years ago. Far before it was surveyed by the Holland Land Company, the region was an active trade route for both settlers and Native Americans. The first settler in Buffalo was in the late 1700s. His name was Joseph Hodges, and he was a unique individual for the area. He was unique in that he had neither red nor white skin. In fact, Hodges was a black man, which confused many, but it made him a good middle man between the natives and settlers. Hodges earned the name "Black Joe," according to the *Buffalonian* in 2003. The number of travelers through the region forced "Black Joe" to educate himself so that he could fluently speak the language used by the Seneca and the other travelers. His mastery allowed him to become an interpreter for many from his small cabin, which became the first tavern in Buffalo. It became a destination where individuals could trade and rest, which is much of what Buffalo has become today.

Buffalo was not always a city. In fact, the region was not surveyed until 1804 by the Holland Land Company. After the survey, settlers began to lay claim to the region. Land was purchased, homes were built and people began to move into the small village. Its name came from the river that ran through the area. The village continued to grow at a slow pace until the War of 1812. In 1813, the British and native troops invaded the village. Historical records state that almost every building in the village was burned to the ground; only two were left standing. Many of the village people were taken to Montreal as captives, while few managed to escape.

The rebuilding of Buffalo was difficult. The region remained very isolated until 1819, when the idea of the "Grand Canal," better known as the Erie Canal, was born. This gave the village of Buffalo the possibility of growth. New harbors and buildings for storage, stores and shops began to be built. People began to move back into the area, and by 1832, banking and insurance companies had moved in, along with breweries. Its access to Lake Erie allowed Buffalo to become one of the largest grain-shipping ports in the world. Buffalo was growing into a place much larger than a village. It would become a city in 1825, and by 1840 there were over eighteen thousand people living here.

Growth didn't slow down; Buffalo continued to boom. European immigrants came to Buffalo to work in the grain mills and steelworks. Industry and manufacturing became one of the key resources for the city. As the population grew, so did the advances that the city experienced. A hospital opened and churches, schools and universities soon followed. A rail line was built through the city to aid in the transportation of goods and people. The city became known as the "City of Light" thanks to neighboring Niagara Falls, which generated hydroelectric power. It was one of the first cities in the United States to have electricity citywide.

Throughout its years, Buffalo has grown with beautiful theatres, historic buildings and artistic beauty. It is a city rich in history, but also given at a price. Buffalo had its own share of class wars in the 1920s, Prohibition challenges in the late 1930s, struggles of the Great Depression and World War II in the 1940s and antiwar movements and riots in the 1960s. The 1970s rejuvenated Buffalo's passion for growth with exciting events such as the opening of the Naval and Serviceman's Park, which features the haunted USS *The Sullivans*; the renovation and reopening of the beautiful Shea's Theatre; and national sports teams teams like the AFC's Buffalo Bills

The USS *The Sullivans*, a haunted monument to Buffalo's past.

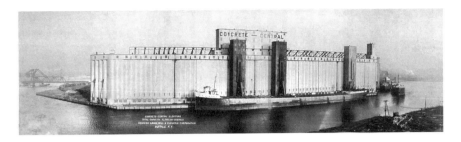

A grain elevator along Buffalo's Lake Erie shoreline. *Courtesy of the Buffalo Historical Society.*

football team and NHL's Buffalo Sabres hockey team. Even with the boom in growth and business surrounding the city, Buffalo still struggled financially due to struggles in the steel and local automotive industry. By the 1980s, the economy had begun to see a gradual improvement. New jobs were created in the region with the opening of the Buffalo/Niagara International Airport. The steel industry gained new guidance and growth, which resulted in unemployment experiencing a steady decline. The retail climate exploded with new shopping malls and stores.

The city itself, from the beginning, has been a city rich in cultures and beauty. It's had its prosperity and its devastation, which leaves it rich in recorded history and even richer in paranormal history. The canal made it very easy to bring in and out many people and cultures and is much of the reason that Buffalo is what it is today. The grain industry is still in use today, though not to the extent of years ago. General Mills and ADM Pillsbury companies still sit on the waterfront. Many of the original grain elevators have begun to deteriorate, though with the help of the historians of the area and the Industrial Heritage Committee of Buffalo, some of the tall elevators have been brought back to their original beauty and use. Even today, you can board the *Miss Buffalo* cruiser ship and take a beautiful journey back through time along the Buffalo River and tour the city ship canal. You can see the beautiful grain and canal buildings that made the little village of Buffalo the massive city that it is today.

GHOST HUNTING—THE BEGINNINGS

The ghost hunting phenomenon first made its presence known in the public mainstream in 1984. Dan Aykroyd and Bill Murray, with a cast of other characters, saddled up with proton packs on their backs and EMF meters to hit the streets of New York City, capturing rampaging ghosts and spirits.

Ghostbusters became a Hollywood blockbuster. It ushered in a new interest in ghost hunting for the general public. Author Vince Wilson points out that prior to 1984, there had never been any mention of using meteorological equipment in the detection of paranormal phenomena. It was only after 1984 that ghost hunters began to use equipment to measure changes in ion counts in the atmosphere, electromagnetic field variations and temperature changes, among many other criteria that are now considered benchmarks in the current field of paranormal investigation. Interest in the paranormal jumped dramatically after the release of the film *White Noise*, which was based on the recording of electronic noise phenomena or ghost voice. Most recently, a flood of paranormal television programs has hit mainstream media. This, however, was not where ghost hunting began.

Ghostly appearances and apparitions have been documented to make appearances to individuals as far back as AD 100. This was actually the first "documented case of paranormal investigation." R.C. Finucane's *Appearances of the Dead: A Cultural History of Ghosts* reports that the case involved a home in Athens, Greece, that was said to be haunted by the spirit of a thin, shackled man. It was said that each night the spirit would rattle its chains at night, bringing disease and sometimes death to the visitors of the home. Not threatened by the spirit, the philosopher Athenodorus purchased the Athens home. As first he tried to ignore the existence of the spirit. As he found ignoring the spirit didn't work, he observed as the spirit beckoned to him. He followed it into the garden of the home, where it promptly vanished. The next day, local officials came and dug at the site where the spirit had vanished, and there they discovered a shackled skeleton. They promptly gave it a proper burial and the haunting stopped.

The first true ghost hunters came shortly after the Fox sisters began the Spiritualist movement. John and Margaret Fox were devout Methodists living in Hydesville, New York, in 1848 when the first events took place. Their four adult children had long since moved away and started families of their own, leaving the youngest daughters, Margaretta and Catherine (Maggie and Kate), in their small home. One night in March, the family was asleep when strange noises abruptly startled them awake. Reportedly, a variety of bangs, raps and similar sounds kept the Fox family up that night and every night for the rest of the week. They searched for, but could not find, a source for the mysterious sounds. On March 31, the date often recognized as the birth of Spiritualism, Kate, the younger of the two girls, decided to try to discover what was causing the rapping. She asked the noise to rap ten times. It did. Kate's questions became more complicated, querying as to the ages of the six Fox children, among other things, and each time the tapping responded perfectly.

The Fox sisters helped to begin the
Spiritualism movement. *Courtesy of Lily
Dale Historical Society.*

Through a series of question and answer sessions with the source, Kate
discovered that the noise was that of the spirit of a peddler who had been
murdered and buried in the basement of the Fox house some years past.
The spiritual communication was given validity when human remains were
reportedly unearthed beneath the floor of the small cottage. As word of the
occurrences spread, the girls gained fame for their discovery of what would
set off a veritable wildfire of Spiritualist activity. The sisters conducted many
sessions outside of their own home as well, including a session in the Hyde
House, better known as the Octagon House, which is now located at the
Genesee Country Village in Mumford, New York.

In April 1848, news of the now locally famous "Hydesville Rappings"
reached the ears of Leah Fox Fish, Maggie and Kate's older sister. Middle-
aged Leah lived with her adolescent daughter in nearby Rochester, New
York. Her husband had abandoned her and her daughter, so when Mrs.
Fish saw the opportunity to capitalize on the fame of her younger sisters, she
decided to seize it. Kate had to move to her brother's house in Auburn, New
York, while Margaret took refuge at her sister Leah's house on Plymouth
Avenue in Rochester. Raps broke out at both places, indicating that it was
the young girls who were supplying the necessary vital energy for the spirit to
manifest as it did. The raps were particularly violent in Leah's house.

The violent disturbances continued in Leah's house until a friend named Isaac Post remembered that the girls' brother, David, had once conversed with the Hydesville spirits using the alphabet. As an experiment, they tried this method again with the following results: "Dear Friends, you must proclaim this truth to the world. This is the dawning of a new era; you must not try to conceal it any longer. When you do your duty God will protect you and good spirits will watch over you."

From that time onward, the communications poured forth and the manifestations were orderly and nonviolent in nature. The successful relaying of the above message apparently released the frustration and urgency on the part of the spirit, thereby allowing more orderly and cohesive communication. Imagine, if you can, the sense of release you would feel if, after trying so very hard to convey a message to someone without success, you were suddenly able to do so. This is exactly what the spirit experienced during this period.

Although later on the Fox sisters would come under considerable heat with allegations of fraud and hoax, these allegations would never be proven without a shadow of a doubt. The commercial successes of this family had led to a much more important element: a way of believing in life after death, or modern Spiritualism. Spiritualism is a philosophy that studies the laws of nature on both the seen and unseen sides of life and bases its conclusions upon present observed facts. It strives to understand the relationship between the physical, spiritual and mental laws of nature that God has put into place. In 1856, Rochester became the home to one of the first Spiritualist churches in the country, built just down the street from the home of Leah Fox.

This emergence of spiritual communication gained the interest of several individuals from the United Kingdom who formed an organization known as the "ghost club," founded in 1862 by two members of the faculty at Cambridge University. Their goal was to expose fraudulent spiritual mediums and investigate authentic psychic and spiritual phenomenon. One of the first investigations they conducted were of the Spiritualists known as the Davenport brothers. The Davenport brothers conducted a process known as spirit paintings. They would place a blank canvas on a stage surrounded by curtains or covered by a cloth. Paints would be placed near the canvas on the floor. As people watched, over the course of little time, masterpieces would be created. What made them unusual was that these masterpieces were created so quickly and with no brush strokes at all. Many of their paintings hang today in the Spiritualist community in Lily Dale, New York. Now the results of their investigation of the Davenport brothers, along with many of their first investigations, are unknown, but their interest in investigating such phenomena caused interest to spread rapidly. It was a select group of individuals that began to attract people such as Charles Dickens, Harry Houdini, Sir Aurthur Conan Doyle and Harry Price, among many others. The organization is still in existence today and is considered the oldest paranormal research organization in the world, according to its website. Today there exist hundreds of ghost-hunting and paranormal investigation organizations across the country, with more doing their own "hunting" independently.

A CRASH COURSE IN GHOST HUNTING

Exploration into the unknown is a compulsion for many. It's that desire to explore, fueled by curiosity and bridled by fear, that drives humanity for answers to questions for which there are none currently. This is what has built the field of paranormal investigation. It's a field with scientists and philosophers working side by side with housewives and maintenance workers. It's a rare field of interest that combines a wide diversity of backgrounds to create a diversity of ideas and thoughts that makes paranormal investigation so wonderful and exciting. One never knows who will be the first to prove the existence of life after death; remember that Einstein himself was a mere custodian to begin with.

If you're just beginning in serious paranormal investigation or hunting ghosts for fun, this guide will provide you with a variety of interesting locales to explore, diving into their history, the stories and even results from some of the researchers who have already visited the location. Before you begin though, there are some tools that you will need to have available to you. Should you decide to use new technology, consider having these items with you:

Flashlight: Flashlights are an important tool in any investigation. The most dangerous aspect of any ghost hunt is the physical environment. It is best to use an LED-based flashlight. They provide a softer light, which reduces the occurrences of nightblindness and light reflection in photographs. Some investigators will use green-colored LED lights to further reduce reflection.

Notebook and Pen: Bring along a journal to keep record of any unexplained phenomena that may occur during the investigation. It can also be useful to draw maps of the location to refer to later during the review of data.

Camera: Investigators tend to each have their own preference as to what type of camera they use during the investigation. The most popular

Paranormal
investigations require
an eye for detail.

formats of cameras are 35mm, digital and Instamatic cameras. Each has its advantages and disadvantages. The researcher using a 35mm camera and Instamatic should utilize a film speed of at least 400ASL or greater during the investigation, with an indirect flash. Truly remarkable photographs have been taken with 35mm cameras, even when they are disposable ones. The Instamatic camera provides immediate results. It provides the researcher also with a film negative for additional proof of any phenomenon when one is captured. The drawbacks to film are the expense and the need to develop it after the investigation. Labs often use their own criteria when developing the film negative, and if the photograph looks too dark or seems to contain an error, they often won't make a print. It is important to ask the lab where the film is dropped off to print every picture on the roll, and some will place them on a CD for you as well. Digital cameras are more often the choice of many investigators because they provide instant results and are more cost-effective. These cameras can "see" in a slightly wider light range than the human eye. As a test, the remote for your television emits an infrared beam. Try this: press a button on your television remote and take a picture of the end of the remote. You won't see the light with your eye but the camera will show the light emitting from the remote. If a researcher uses a digital camera, it is important to use a camera of at least six megapixels at the highest quality setting. Lower-quality cameras can often create "data errors" on the image, causing false images to appear. The drawback to the digital camera is skepticism. If a researcher is able to capture a remarkable image, there may be a question to its authenticity because of the advent of photo-editing software.

Audio Recorder: There are two types of recorders that can be used in paranormal investigation: digital and analog. The preference really depends upon the individual. Audio recorders are useful in recording notes and observations about the haunted location, but sometimes they pick up just a little bit more. Many times audio recorders that are used in spiritually active locations will uncover a surprise when the recording is reviewed—the voice of a ghost.

These voices will not be heard at the time of recording but will only be heard upon its playback. These are usually simple, one-word responses or short phrases, recorded well above or below the range of human hearing. This is known as electronic voice phenomenon, or EVP. There are some simple guidelines to follow when recording electronic voice phenomena, and these include: ask simple questions, pause between questions, record in short sessions, don't whisper, record on the highest quality and review the recording with headphones. The headphones allow the researcher to hear more subtle sounds. If magnetic or analog tape is used, record on only one side. If both sides are used, there may be bleed through from the opposite side, causing "false ghost voices." Cassette tapes no longer than forty-five minutes per side should be used, since longer tapes may stretch, and only brand-name cassettes should be used. The generic cassettes sold are actually recycled tape, which may not be completely erased, again causing false ghost voices. Audio recorders have the ability to also record slightly outside the range of human hearing.

Video Recorder: The preferred video camcorders to use with ghost hunting are the Sony-brand cameras. These cameras have the unique "night shot" feature, which allows for video recording in complete darkness. The camera emits a light on the infrared light spectrum that it uses to record. The infrared light illuminates the area and yet is not visible by the human eye. The advantage to using a camera sensitive to infrared light is that it is believed that ghosts or spirits are energy forms that exist on that wavelength of light. This allows the opportunity for forms or movements not visible to the human eye to be captured. When recording, it is important to use slow movements and be conscious of all the surroundings because even with infrared light there can be light reflection. Light reflection can sometimes present false ghost images. Keep in mind that even though video is being recorded, so is audio. Camcorders often record very high-quality EVPs.

EMF Meter: EMF meters are used to measure variations in the electric fields in an environment. These measure changes in the magnetic, AC and DC spectrums of energy. Investigators are looking for unexplained spikes in energy when using these instruments. Since it is theorized that ghosts or spirits are composed of energy, it is believed that these meters would register changes in the environment if there was paranormal activity.

As recently as twenty years ago, many of these instruments were not available to people interested in researching paranormal phenomena. So what did they use? They used some old-school techniques that can still be used today, even together with the newer technology.

Compass: A simple compass works as effectively as an EMF meter. While holding a compass or placing it on a hard surface, watch the needle. It will point due north. When there are changes in the magnetic field, the compass will respond and react. Watch for the needle to begin to swing and change directions independently and then take a photograph in that direction. You may be surprised at what you discover. The change in the needle direction demonstrates that there is a closer magnetic field influencing the needle, hence a ghost.

Pendulum: Pendulums have been used as a form of spirit communication and energy dowsing for centuries. They can be made of any type of material. Some people use crystals, a metal weight or wood at the end of a chain. The pendulum's chain is held between the thumb and index finger with the arm steadied. The statement is then made to "show me 'no'"; watch as the pendulum responds. For some it will swing back and forth and for others it will spin in a circle. The question is then asked to "show me 'yes,'" and a different response will occur. This is establishing the baseline movements for answers that allows for spirit communications.

Dowsing Rods: Not just used for looking for water, dowsing rods can also be used in much the same way as a pendulum. The most commonly used dowsing rods in ghost hunting tend to be made of coat hanger–type material and are lightly held in the hand. The user establishes yes and no responses as he does with the pendulum. One response will cross the rods and another will open them. The advantage to dowsing rods is that they can be used to direct the investigator to the spirit in the area. When asked, the rods will point to the direction. As the dowser gets closer, the rods begin to converge, crossing completely in front of the spirit.

Trust your senses: They are as old as humanity and once were used for survival. If you feel like someone is watching you in a certain direction, take a picture. Trust your senses. You will be surprised at what you may capture.

Now you're all geared up and ready to walk behind the veil and into the world of ghost hunting. Use this book as your guide to paranormal investigation of the Buffalo area, but remember to do it with respect and reverence. Show respect for the spirits as you would for a living person. Ask permission before going onto any private property. Remember that most cemeteries close at dusk, but realize that paranormal activity can happen at any point of the day.

BEDS, "SPOOKS" AND "SPIRITS"

Food critics have best described Buffalo as a melting pot of cuisine. The diverse population of the city brings a wide range of food choices. It's not unusual to discover restaurant upon restaurant serving authentic Polish and Italian dishes to specialties from Germany, Greece and India. Buffalo's variety of food is only matched by its selection of elegant lodging, from unique bed-and-breakfast accommodations to lavish hotels, which makes for an exciting night life for both the living and the dead.

DOCK AT THE BAY

3800 Hoover Drive, Blasdell, New York
www.DockAtTheBay.com

Soldiers in uniform are said to be walking the hallways of this popular Buffalo dining destination. Today, a beautiful panoramic overview of the bay is what visitors to Dock at the Bay will experience, but some two hundred years ago, it was a bay filled with commerce, trading vessels and warships. The bay became an essential military point during the War of 1812, providing a stop for ships and their crews. Today's Dock at the Bay was formerly known as the WillLink Hotel and became a popular place for soldiers during the war.

One local legend tells of Captain James Byrd, who served on one of Admiral Perry's ships during the war. He would set his ship to anchor at this point in the bay and sneak off ship to rendezvous with a lady friend late at night. They met at the WillLink Hotel. He would then return early in the morning, to no one's suspicion. One night, Byrd was seen coming back onboard the ship. He was soon after court-martialed and shot by a firing squad. His body was laid to rest in Hamburg, New York.

The Dock at the Bay, where past soldiers continue to roam.

Employee Carl Mazzu believes that the spirit of the captain still walks in the building. He recalls one encounter when he had just finished work for the night. As he was preparing to leave, he heard the sound of heavy footsteps on the floor. He described them as boot heels—heavy boots pacing the floor above him. It would go from one end of the building to the other. When he went to investigate, no one was there. Several employees have had similar experiences at the Dock at the Bay throughout the years. One evening after a banquet, when guests were leaving, a waitress noticed a tall man wearing a black hat and long jacket who stood by one of the serving tables. As she watched, the man turned and "floated" up the stairs to the banquet room. A few moments later, the disc jockey came running down the stairs, scared out of his mind. He told the waitress that a man had just come up the stairs to the room and, as he watched, evaporated before his eyes. To this day, the disc jockey has not returned to the restaurant, according to Mason Winfield's television documentary *The Phantom Tour: The 13 Most Haunted Places in Western New York*. Another disc jockey tells of coming into work early one day to set up for a party in the banquet room. Once this task was completed, he headed downstairs to get dressed for the party. He returned to the banquet room to do his sound check before any quests arrived, only to hear a voice quietly whisper his name, "James." He looked around and no one was there. He walked closer to his equipment to hear "James" called a little louder. Puzzled, he continued to his table to hear his name yelled: "James!" He turned quickly around to see no one in the room. Perhaps this was the gentle whisper of the girlfriend still looking for her captain.

Locals believe that there are two Byrds whose spirits still haunt the Dock at the Bay. The other is that of Amos Byrd, who fought in the War of 1812 at the Battle of Black Rock. His grave is not far from the restaurant. As the story goes, there was a scuffle in the tavern in the mid-1800s. The barkeep instructed the men to take it outside, where it became more heated. Gunshots were fired that missed the men, but one bullet hit the gravestone of Amos Byrd, knocking a small piece off of it. It is said that in the fight, a piece of the steps to the tavern was broken off as well. The two men who fought are said to have taken the piece of stone from Byrd's grave marker and placed it into the crack in the steps of the tavern to repair it. Some believe that Byrd is upset that his rest was disturbed so haunts the bay. Today, things will fall off the tables with no explanation and empty pitchers will fly across the kitchen with no one near. Many believe that they have to be careful of what they say or do at the Dock at the Bay so they don't upset the spirits.

GRAND ISLAND HOLIDAY INN

100 White Haven Road, Grand Island, New York
www.MyHolidayInn.com

One of the more famous haunts of Buffalo is the Grand Island Holiday Inn. Many believe the Holiday Inn to be haunted by the young five-year-old spirit whom the hotel staff have affectionately named Tanya. The spirit of Tanya is said to run up and down the hallways late at night at the hotel with the sounds of a ball bouncing. There have even been accounts of guests experiencing the sensation of the beds "bouncing" at night, as if someone were jumping on them. Tanya is believed to be the spirit of a young girl who died in a house fire in the 1800s; the hotel was built on the ashes of the home, according to Lynda Lee Macken's book *New York State's Haunted Landmarks*. According to historical records, this story isn't possible. Local historian Teddy Linenfelser tells that a home was indeed built on the property in the early 1830s. It was purchased in 1848 by the town supervisor, John Nice, who raised ten children there, none of whom had the name Tanya. There are no records of the home ever burning down. It was later sold and became a restaurant for several years. In 1962, the restaurant burned down and the property was then purchased by the hotel. How does this account for the young child spirit that roams the building? It doesn't, but that doesn't mean that the spirit doesn't exist. Consider that the story may just be wrong.

One evening, guests came down to the main desk. They seemed quite upset and began to complain that the person behind the desk must have put two families in the same room by accident. As they had walked into their room after coming from dinner, they had seen a young girl in the room playing with their children's toys that had been left there. As the guests began to explain what the little girl looked like, the hotel clerk stopped them and asked, "You're in room 422, right?" They responded, "Why yes." They were a bit puzzled because they hadn't shared the room number yet. He went on to explain that they had just met Tanya, one of the ghost guests of the hotel. They were promptly placed in another room.

A former employee of the hotel recalled arriving for work one morning. He came in about 5:00 a.m. and stopped at the coffee shop. He recalled what a beautiful morning it was, with the sun rising and glistening off the water of the lake. This was routine for him every morning and was his way to relax a bit before the hectic day began. This morning had started out just like every other, except that he noticed a young girl playing down in the grass wearing a white nightgown. His first thoughts were that someone's child had sneaked out of their room and out of the hotel. He grabbed his keys and headed down to the porch to see whose child it was. As he walked outside, the girl was standing and had begun to walk toward one of the older buildings, a smokehouse over two hundred years old. He called to her. She turned and gave him a smile but continued walking. She turned the corner of the smokehouse with the employee following quickly behind. When he rounded the corner she was gone—she had vanished. He circled the building but could not find a sign of anyone. The little girl had just disappeared.

The spirit of Tanya isn't the only one said to haunt the Grand Island Holiday Inn, although she is the most famous. A former manager of the Holiday Inn explains that one evening he was in his office and had a frightening encounter. He glanced up from his work in the late-night hours to see the shadow of a tall man before him. He was walking back and forth in the hallway in front of his door and wearing an 1800s fashion cape or long coat with a tall stovepipe hat. Guests have also reported this same man in room 422.

Psychics who have visited the property feel that there are at least four or five entities that are active at the hotel. What makes the hotel such a hotbed of paranormal activity? It is really anyone's, guess but it seems that it's the place to stay for a "spirited" adventure.

Mansion on Delaware Avenue

414 Delaware Avenue, Buffalo, New York

In 1869, Charles Sternberg commissioned architect George Allison to build him a mansion. There is little known about Allison other than the fact that he was the designer of many of the high-priced mansions that were constructed along Delaware Avenue. Sternberg was one of the grain tycoons who took up residence in the city of Buffalo. Unfortunately, he never saw the completion of his home before his death. The home showcases over twenty thousand square feet of living space with eighteen-foot ceilings and over two hundred windows, including several twelve-foot-tall bay windows that flood the interior with light. The massive number of windows in the home has earned the mansion the name the "house of light." The light not only floods into it during the day, but in the darkness of night, it illuminates all that is around it.

After Sternberg's death, the mansion was purchased by Samuel Curtis Trubee, who converted the space into a one-hundred-room hotel. It was open in time to operate during the Pan-American Exposition, which flooded visitors into the region. Trubee's hotel was filled to the maximum, charging the highest price in the city, three dollars a night. The spillover guests were allowed to sleep in the yard around the home. The hotel flourished through the years, including during the Great Depression, when local rumors had it that the mansion also served as a high-class bordello.

World War II ended and restaurant entrepreneur Hugo DiGuilio bought the establishment and opened the restaurant Victor Hugo Wine Cellars, which operated until the mid-1970s. The building remained abandoned until 2001, when the Mansion of Delaware Avenue opened its doors, offering twenty-eight luxury suites with butler service for every visitor, a unique feature to Buffalo accommodations. This elegant hotel also offers something else very special for its visitors: a few spirits of the past that still remain and linger.

Hotel staff and guests have reported seeing the spirit of a little girl that runs throughout the hotel. She stands out because her clothing is that of the nineteenth century. Her voice is often heard being carried down the hallways, laughing and singing little girls' games. She is a friendly spirit looking for someone to play with. No one is certain who this little girl is; perhaps she is an energy imprint of a past guest or even the child of one of the past owners. Other reports at the hotel include one from one morning when a house cleaner had stepped into a room briefly to check its vacancy. She returned to the hallway to find her cart flipped over with all of its contents thrown about the hall. She went back into the room and called to report the incident to her supervisor, but upon returning to the hallway moments later, her cart was back upright with everything in its place. The mansion definitely has a variety of paranormal activity for its guests. There are some who claim to have seen orbs of light with their eyes and elevators that open and close by themselves. One has to wonder, who are truly the guests in this home? Are they the visiting guests or the spirits themselves?

MILL GLENN INN BED—AND—BREAKFAST

102 Pletcher Road, Youngstown, New York

The Mill Glenn Inn is located in what is considered one of western New York's most haunted regions: the town of Lewiston. During the War of 1812, British troops were ordered to burn the town of Lewiston as retaliation against the doings of General McClure, an American general. The residents of the town were ordered to leave and the town was burned to the ground, leaving women and children to try to survive a brutal winter homeless. The retaliation for the burning was swift and savage by the British and Native Americans. In the end, a vast majority of the residents of Lewiston had perished and only one building remained standing. Many times it is emotionally charged events like this that hold on to psychic energy, allowing spirits to remain or even to draw spirits back in.

Once a dairy farm, the Mill Glenn Inn Bed-and-Breakfast has two resident spirits. One is that of a feline phantom and the other an elderly gentleman. A prior owner shared her first experience at the inn. Shortly after she had purchased the property, she encountered a cat in the house. It was a dark gray cat, and as she watched it, it walked through the kitchen, up the stairs and into the bathroom. When the owner went into the bathroom, the cat had vanished. Several days later, she saw the dark cat again in the home, but this time her dogs noticed it too. Not being brave dogs, they just watched the cat walk up the stairs. The owner followed again, only to have it vanish. Although she had only canines for witnesses, this time she knew that she wasn't seeing things and called the prior owner to ask her about a cat in the house. The prior owner explained that she had a cat in the home and described the phantom feline exactly. When asked how old the cat was, the prior owner broke down and explained that she had just died the week prior. It seems that the cat's litter box was once kept in the upstairs bathroom.

One morning, two guests came down for breakfast. They were travelers through the area and it was their first time staying at the bed-and-breakfast. As breakfast was being served, they asked if another guest wouldn't be joining them. They had heard the voice of an older gentleman in the hallway several times the prior night and thought it would be nice to meet him. The innkeeper explained that they were the only guests in the home that night. They went on to explain that they had heard him talking but couldn't make out what he was saying. They could even hear his footsteps down the hallway, but the innkeeper insisted that no one else had been there. A few days later, the owners were enjoying a quiet night without guests when the events with their guests began to make sense. As they sat in the living room, they began to hear the sound of footsteps walking back and forth on the floor above them in the bedroom, the floorboards creaking with each step. When they investigated, there was no one there. It seems that even ghosts need a little vacation once in a while.

ROYCROFT INN

40 South Grove Street East Aurora, New York
www.RoycroftInn.com

In 1895, the Roycroft community was formed by Elbert Hubbard. It was to be a completely self-contained arts and crafts community. It drew such well-known names as Frank Lloyd Wright and Gustav Stickley to work. It quickly became a mecca for those interested in the arts and crafts movement. In 1905, the Roycroft Inn was opened to accommodate the thousands of visitors who journeyed to East Aurora. Today, it still greets visitors to this historic village with a flavor of the past. There are twenty-eight guestrooms, each decorated in the arts and crafts style of the time. There is also a fine dining restaurant, event rooms and, of course, "finer spirits."

As legend has it, Hubbard was a world traveler. In the last years of his life, he traveled with his wife to Germany. On May 15, 1915, they boarded a United Kingdom–bound ocean liner from New York. While just off the coast of France, a German U-boat sunk the ship. Hubbard did not survive. Since that day, the spirit of Hubbard has been seen in Ireland, France and

The Roycroft Inn.

at the Roycroft Inn. According to an article in the October 2008 *Buffalo Downtowner*, there is one gentleman who claims to have frequent conversations with Hubbard at the inn. He speaks directly to the portrait of him behind the bar. There have also been reports of Hubbard walking down the street speaking to another gentleman, in the inn walking down the stairs and reading in the Ruskin Room.

THIRTY MILE POINT LIGHTHOUSE

9701 Lower Lake Road, Barker, New York

There is a place along the Niagara River just south of Buffalo that has claimed many ships over the past three hundred years. In 1780, the HMS *Ontario* sank here. Local legend says that the ship was carrying British troops and over $15,000 in British payroll. In 1817, the *Mary* sank in the same area. Historical records show that some seventeen years after the sinking, neighbors to the area witnessed men rowing to shore on a boat. They walked up to the

Spirits are forever watchful from the Thirty Mile Point Lighthouse. *Courtesy of the U.S. Coast Guard.*

top of the hill and began to dig. They returned to their rowboat with a chest and rowed back out to the ship waiting in the river. The locals believed that the men came to retrieve the treasure left by crew of the *Mary*. Is it local legend? Perhaps. But there have been many documented ships sinking in this area of the Niagara River, which is why the Thirty Mile Point Lighthouse was built in 1875 just off the river to mark a dangerous sandbar.

The lighthouse stands seventy feet tall and is made completely of limestone. The light in the house was fueled by kerosene until 1885, when it became one of the first lighthouses in the United States to be electric. The beam of light showed upward of sixteen miles. The lighthouse remained in operation until 1958, when the sandbar no longer posed a threat. It was turned over to the New York State Department of Parks and Recreation for preservation by the United States Coast Guard. Today it serves as a historic landmark of times long past and is the centerpiece of Golden Hill State Park. It is one of the few remaining lighthouses that allow guests to spend the night.

As you flip through the guestbooks at the Thirty Mile Point Lighthouse, you certainly see exclamations of people's wonderful stays and the beautiful accommodations, but there is something else that you wouldn't expect: the mention of ghosts. Guests have told of their television turning on or off by itself and strange noises that come from the kitchen. An older gentleman dressed in early 1900s clothing is said to walk the property, still taking care of the house. Guests have reported nights where he walks into their room, sits down on the bed and vanishes. A woman often appears in the kitchen. She seemingly is going through the drawers, looking confused and dazed. Maintenance workers share stories of footsteps walking on the floor above them, and when they investigate, no one is there.

WESTERN HOUSE

210 West Main Street, Springville, New York

Springville, New York, sits about thirty miles south of Buffalo. It is a village rich in beauty and history. Nestled into the center of the village's historic district is a building that has withstood many changes, owners and mysteries. This building is known as the Western House, and it has kept that name since it was built in 1884 as a hospitality house for the Mangus Beck Brewing Company and Bottling Works. As this massive building sits right on the rail line that was originally the Buffalo, Rochester & Pittsburgh, it was usually very busy and saw many faces. Throughout the years, this three-story building has been many things, from hotels to saloons, the stage of a brutal murder and the mysterious piece to one of western New York's most mindboggling cold cases.

After the brewing works sold the Western House to private ownership, it was bought and taken over by the Sieder family. The Western House was also known after that by the names of Sieder Hotel and the Sieder Tavern. As the Sieder family ran the establishment, the family grew around them. The family also had the Pennsylvania Gasoline and Kerosene Delivery business, which was located in a small building right behind the Western House. It wasn't until almost a century later that they found the other useful purpose for that business.

The mysteries started around the turn of the nineteenth century. In the summer of 1906, a few men sat around in the tavern playing cards. A win or loss resulting in a small rift between the men ended in a small dispute, and everyone parted ways for the evening. The next night, three of the men were enjoying the Sieder Hotel until the young hours of the morning. When the bar closed for the night, the men sat out on the veranda for some time enjoying the beautiful summer night, and then decided to head home. Fred Percival, Fred Schneider and William Deet had no idea what

The Western House.

was ahead of them. It is said that their small rift from the previous night caught up with them. As William Deet escaped injury, he described the incident as follows. The three men had set out for home for the evening when a man jumped out from between the freight cars and began shooting at them. The man fired six shots and fled the scene. Fred Percival was shot in the breast and Fred Schnieder was hit once in the leg and once in the stomach. William Deet escaped without harm, but it is said that he was almost struck in the head with a bullet. After the shooting occurred, Fred Percival staggered his way across the road and stumbled into the hotel, made it to the second floor and crumbled into a close friend's room, for at that time, the Western House had become a boardinghouse. His last words included the statement, "Haber did it."

Now with there being two Habers in the Springville area at the time, the police made quick duty to set out a search for the brothers. The two men happened to live together, as Martin Haber, thirty-two, boarded with his older brother Peter, who was thirty-six years old, married and had four children. The police flew through the home and only found the older brother, who was asleep with his family and had no knowledge of what had happened. Who they didn't locate was Martin, the younger brother. As the police continued their search, they came across a witness by the name of L.L. Baily who noted that when he heard shots coming from the area, he went to see what had happened. He came across Martin Haber reloading a revolver and was immediately attacked by the man with the revolver under his nose. Martin mumbled something like, "Get out o this!" and Mr. Baily ran, not looking back. It is supposed to this day that, despite the efforts of the police department in Springville and surrounding areas, Martin Haber escaped in the direction of Ellicotville by train within a few hours of the incident. The headline for the *Springville Journal* the next day says it all: "Whiskey and Cards the Cause of It." So a card game gone bad sent one man to his grave and almost another. The Sieder Hotel was the battlefield of a deadly shootout.

Some years later, in October 1936, the body of a young girl was found on the Seneca Indian Reservation in Cattaraugus. Christiana Mary Jureller's body was found badly beaten with many broken bones. It would seem that the woman was beaten to death. In the small cove of trees off the road where she was found, there were no signs of a disturbance on the ground, which left police very baffled. The only thing found was impressions of

Sharlean Curtis recalls the murder that happened.

footprints walking up the banks from her high heels, as though she walked to the scene of her death. There were no discrepancies on the ground or surrounding areas. With many efforts to find the girl's identity, there was finally a correct match given by her father, Leonard Jureller, and married sisters, Mrs. Harry Prentice and Mrs. Sylvester Smith. When asked about the woman's home life, the police were told that she was not a woman who dated and she stayed home, as she was very close to her disabled mother. When the sisters found out that their deceased sister was six months pregnant, they were very shocked.

Originally, Christiana Mary Jureller had told her family that she would be taking a train out to Buffalo to see some family members. Harry Prentice, her brother-in-law, agreed to take her to the station so she could get on her way. After that there were many reports of some people seeing her and others not seeing her. The police had a very hard time trying to figure out if the young woman had even boarded the train. You can only imagine how surprised the police were to find out that another sister of Christiana Mary Jureller's, Helen, had disappeared six years earlier, never to be found. When her case was looked into after the death of Christiana, it was found that Harry Prentice, on the police force at the time, had often entered through the back door of the inn where Helen waitressed and watched her from a secluded telephone booth. It was also rumored that the reason Helen lost her job was that she was noticeably pregnant and could no longer waitress. There were a few instances when Harry, being the brother-in-law of this beautiful, full of life twenty-two-year-old, had refused to let her date or see other men. It was also noted that, when on shift, Harry was often in the area of the Melba Inn in New Cannon. A story was recalled about one night when the young Helen was driven home after work by a guest as an honest favor. When the car arrived at the young girl's home, Harry Prentice was waiting in the driveway, and he pulled her out of the car by her neck as punishment for driving home with another man. Shortly after that, the young girl was driven to the train station by her brother-in-law and never seen again. After a depressed telegram was sent to the family, it was thought that she committed suicide.

After these two cases were melded together, the police targeted Harry Prentice. When questioned of his whereabouts on the day that Christiana Jureller had met her end, he told the police that he had been in the Seider Hotel (the Western House). For most of the day, he gave very specific times and people who could be used as witnesses. He gave a pretty decent alibi about his events of the night, but not a complete one. Most of the witnesses mentioned by Harry Prentice gave stable statements to back up his story, though there were others who couldn't recall him being at the Sieder Hotel that night. Though other clues led to Harry Prentice, the case was never solved. To this day, there is speculation over whether the girl really was killed in the wooded area off Southern Boulevard on the Seneca Indian Reservation or murdered somewhere else. Christiana Jureller was spotted in Buffalo, and the police had somewhat of a description of the car she had been seen riding in. Did she ever board the train? Was her life brought to an end somewhere else? The world may never know, though on the night of her death, Harry Prentice sat in the Western House on and off for the night. Who knows where the beautiful expecting mother met her terrible demise?

Throughout the years, the Western House has known many owners. After the Sieders sold the property, it often became a custom to see the spirit of an older woman roaming the hotel. When Mark Steffan, previous owner until approximately 1999, started to dig up some history of the building, he found that the woman who was often seen by guests and tenants was none other than Christiana Sieder, the wife of Joesph Sieder. Along with the other members of the family, she spent much of her time there. When tearing down the building directly behind the Western House that was used by the Sieder Hotel for Pennsylvania Gas and Kerosene, he also found a hidden room below the floor. After some research was conducted, Steffan found out that the gas business was also used during Prohibition; there was a false bottom on the delivery truck so that drivers could park the truck over the hidden entrance to the lower room of the building and load liquor undetected! Mark Steffan was known to give ghostly tours of the Western House when he owned and operated it. He also made a very large contribution to the historical society upon his moving out of state and selling the business.

Another owner throughout the years, somewhat in the later 1990s, died at the bottom of the master staircase in the Western House of a heart attack. Today's Western House is still very original, with many of the same fixtures and wall hangings that have been purposely preserved over the years. The Western House is still in operation by owner Sharlean Curtis, who has had the business for ten years. She has mentioned that some of her tenants in the upstairs apartments have heard thumping and banging coming from above for no apparent reason. She also told of an older female tenant some years ago who complained of seeing a face appear in her apartment. The woman was not a tenant for very long!

When questioning a past tenant, and father of a current tenant, he reported that he had many problems with activity when living in the upper apartments of the Western House. Who knows who may be roaming these halls at night; could it be Christiana Sieder? Could it be Fred Percival,

The spirit of Christiana Sieder, who still haunts the Western House. *Courtesy of David Batterson.*

who perished in one of the second-story rooms? Could it be the beautiful Christiana Mary Juleller? No one may ever find out. One thing is for certain: there is plenty of activity throughout this beautiful historic building.

WINERY AT MARJIM MANOR

7171 East Lake Road, Appleton, New York
www.MarjimManor.com

Today, Marjim Manor is the destination for over ten thousand visitors annually who make the trek for fine New York State wines and a taste of history that began long before residents began to make wine and long before its six hundred acres of apple orchards were planted. It was even long before the the manor itself was built. The story begins as early as 1826 with a man named William Morgan.

William Morgan was a resident of Batavia, New York. He was originally from Virigina but moved to Batavia in 1824, where he attempted to join the local Masons' lodge. Morgan claimed that he had already been inducted into the Masons in another country. His knowledge of the Masons' secret rituals seemed to demonstrate this, but his application into the lodge was rejected. In his outrage, Mason threatened to publish the secrets of the

Masons and conspired with a local printer, David Miller. The publisher's office mysteriously burned down and Morgan was arrested shortly after for allegedly not paying bills. Miller paid his bail to have him released, but later that day Morgan was arrested again for failure to pay another bill, this time in Canandaguia. A gentleman claiming to be a friend of Morgan's paid his bail and ushered him into a carriage waiting for him outside the jail. Some accounts state that Morgan was very hesitant about getting into the carriage, and many people heard him calling for help. The story becomes at best sketchy after the carriage leaves Canandaguia, but the one fact known is that it was bound for Canada so that Morgan could avoid prison. On its way to Canada, the carriage made a stop at Fort Niagara, where several Masons boarded a boat with Morgan bound for Canada. Legend has it that Morgan was tied to a rock and thrown overboard into the Niagara River. A five-hundred-pound stone marks the location where, on that fateful day in 1826, Morgan died just off the shore of where Marjim Manor now sits.

In 1834, the small parcel of land was purchased by Subell Merritt. Merritt built a 9,500-square-foot manor with each stone imported from Italy. He called the home Appleton Manor. His love of the home brought it to life with gardens, orchards and a special stone garden that he placed around the natural marker of Morgan's death site. Merritt lived in the manor with his four children. Legend has it that one day Merritt was cleaning his gun and his son Lewis walked into the room. Startled, Merritt turned to face Lewis and the gun went off, shooting his son. Lewis died there in the doorway. Merritt ordered that that the doors to that room be closed forever and they were sealed shut. A few years later, Merritt passed away himself. Although there are differing accounts of his passing, the one consistent fact was that he died on a Thursday at 3:00 p.m. After Merritt's death, his daughter, Phoebe Sophia, and her husband moved into the home. One day, the French doors that had been sealed shut for so many years flew wide open. With a gasp, Phoebe Sophia dropped to the floor and died. It was a Thursday afternoon at 3:00 p.m. The family moved out of the manor shortly after, and it was left to deteriorate and decay.

In 1867, the manor was rented by a man by the name of John Morely. He was only there a short time before it was discovered that he had died in the home. His body was found at 3:00 p.m. on a Thursday. In 1895, Dr. Charles Ring purchased the manor. Ring was the director of the Buffalo Insane Asylum. He lived in the manor with his fiancée, Estelle Morse. One year after they moved into the manor, the servants heard a loud bang. They found Ring's body on the floor where he had died. It was 3:00 p.m. on a Thursday. Morse lived in the home until her death many years later. Upon her passing, the manor was purchased by the Sisters of St. Joseph and was used as a summer retreat for them. They often had children from the school running around the grounds and in the manor. One of the favorite companions of the children was a dog named Luke. One day Luke was lying near the fireplace in the manor. He stood up and moved toward the French doors, barked a few times, laid down and died, according to a 2008 article in the *Tonawanda News.* Now much of this sounds like urban legend built up over the years, but is it really?

Winery owner Margo Sue Bittner doesn't feel that it is. There have been records of the haunting of the manor that stretch over the past hundred years. She has personally experienced some of the friendly ghosts at the manor, as have many of her guests. She explains that there are several spirits that she feels wander the ground of the manor. In the yard, psychics have felt the spirit of William Morgan wandering the shoreline. Bittner recalls that one day when she was talking about the ghosts at the manor, a bottle of wine fell off one of the shelves to the floor. As she looked, it was laid on its side and then sat straight up. The bottle that had fallen was the one that was dedicated to the memory of Subell Merritt. There have been other accounts of the French doors blowing open spontaneously. Wind could often account for this, if they didn't just happen to blow open at 3:00 p.m. on Thursdays. Other accounts that people have reported have included the sound of footsteps on the porch. Legend has it that Merritt still wanders the manor looking for his son. Stereos turn on by themselves and people feel a presence watching them. A male figure has been spotted in the upstairs of the manor. A candle flicker has often been seen from the copula of the manor late at night.

The winery at Marjim Manor asked Western New York Paranormal to investigate the sightings of ghosts on the manor grounds in the fall of 2005. The team stationed infrared cameras along the porch, along with audio recorders, in an attempt to capture any recordings of potential ghost voices in the form of electronic voice phenomena. A small mobile team worked its way through the home taking photographs, temperature readings and attempting to pick up psychic impressions. In the basement, the team could feel a heavy presence. It was nothing negative, just a strong energy force. At one point, a team member stated that something touched him and at that time a sudden temperature drop was recorded. Several photographs were taken but due to the high dust content of the area, they had to be disregarded as any form of evidence. The most activity in the manor that evening seemed to be located on the higher floors, where the family resides. The higher the team members moved in the building, the stronger the energy became. They had the opportunity to spend some time in the cupola, where they conducted an intensive audio recording session. The psychic asked, "Who's here?" and a response was heard on the recording afterward of a female saying, "I am." He asked, "Why are you up here?" She responded, "'Cause I can see better." A cupola is also known as a widow's walk. Was this the spirit of Estelle waiting for the return of her husband? Who knows for certain, but the fact that there are "spirits" at the Winery at Marjim Manor is.

CREEPY CEMETERIES

Cemeteries—are they haunted places, or is it just our minds' overactive imaginations? It seems that every town has local legends and lore about a spooky cemetery. Some legends tell of the phantom hitchhiker or fabled woman in white, while others describe hell hounds that howl at the moon and murderous spirits lurking in the shadows. Buffalo is no different. This old city has its share of fabled haunted resting places…

BUFFUM STREET CEMETERY

Buffum Street, West Seneca, New York

The Buffum Street Cemetery was named after the original owners of the property who were laid to rest here. In the 1800s, it was common practice to name the cemetery after the landowners, but it is not them who remain the active souls in this cemetery. Those spirits have perhaps a much farther away home that began in Mount Morris, New York. The city of Rochester and the Genesee Valley experienced great floods during the 1800s. They were documented to happen every seven years from 1865 to 1950. The U.S. Army Corps of Engineers began development of a dam in the town of Mount Morris to correct the problem. In doing this, the flow of a portion of the Genesee River would need to be changed. It would now go directly through a parcel of land that was a Native American burial ground. The remains were removed and placed in the Buffum Street Cemetery; among those remains were those of Chief Red Jacket and Mary Jemison, who was a white woman adopted as a child by the Seneca. The move, however, was not complete. According to local legends, some bones were missing. What remained of Red Jacket and Jemison was later moved again. Red Jacket was laid to rest in Forest Lawn Cemetery, while Jemison was returned to rest at Letchworth State Park.

Neighbors of the cemetery have reported unexplained phenomenon many times. In their own homes, objects would move on their own, and shadowy figures would be seen walking through their homes. Electrical problems became common occurrences, with lights turning on and off, batteries draining quickly and televisions turning on by themselves. Strangest of all, perhaps, was how the animals reacted around the area. Dogs would snarl and growl at wide open areas, backing away from something unseen, according to the 2008 *Buffalo Downtowner.*

Could what remains restless at the Buffum Street Cemetery be the spirits of the Native Americans who were transplanted? Could it perhaps even be the spirits of Red Jacket or Jemison? No one will ever know for certain, but one has to question what influence it really does have on the spirits that have passed when their remains are disturbed so many times.

COLD SPRINGS BURIAL GROUNDS

Chestnut and Cold Springs Roads, Lockport, New York

Along this abandoned stretch of road in Lockport, New York, passersby will encounter an area where the road divides a small cemetery. Stones from the cemetery lay on each side of the road. Since 1900, local legends tell of an apparition that haunts the roadway. Those who have encountered the spirit describe it as taking the form of an elderly woman who stands alongside the road. It is believed that this is the spirit of a deranged woman who used to wander the area in the late 1800s, as she often enjoyed nighttime walks. In a local paper, it was reported that she would often walk up to women and pull their hats down over their faces and yank on their hair. Many in the area believed that she suffered from mental illness.

Near the cemetery is a small bridge where many have encountered the apparition. In one account, two local teens were driving down the road one evening when they were forced to stop by a figure standing in the middle of the road. The teenagers became so scared that they drove off the road and hit the stone cemetery wall. Other accounts have also occurred in the same area with people driving through a figure and causing it no harm, while others have swerved to miss her. There have been two reported accidents, according to a Niagara County sheriff's deputy. In light of the accidents, the bridge was kept under observation, and one night a deputy apprehended the woman. On the way to the police station, she vanished from the back of the patrol car.

In an eyewitness account, Rod McKeowon described a rainy night when he was on his way home. He was driving down the road when he saw a woman walking on the opposite side of the road in the rain. He described her as in her mid-twenties, having long blonde hair and wearing a black shirt and pants, but no shoes. What made her stick out to him was the fact that she seemed illuminated by her own light. As he passed her, she turned to look at him, but she had no face. McKeowon slammed on his brakes and looked in his rear-view mirror but she had already vanished.

Is the phantom of Cold Springs just an urban legend that has changed through time or are there multiple entities that wander the road?

ELM LAWN CEMETERY

3939 Delaware Avenue, Kenmore, New York
www.ElmLawnCemetery.com

Elm Lawn Cemetery was originally a parcel of land owned by the Shell family. Their family had a farm that covered over 163 acres in the early 1800s. As was common in that era, the family often buried their dead on their own property. A small family grave site was placed on the land as the family members passed away. After the last member passed, the farm passed into the hands of Judge George Lewis and the plots remained undisturbed. Since there were graves on the property, it became difficult to obtain a clear title for the land, so the bodies were removed and placed in the Faling Cemetery down the road. The property was eventually turned over to the Buffalo Burial Park Association and was turned into the Elm Lawn Cemetery about 1901. The Shell family members were then returned to Elm Lawn and placed back into their original burial sites, which remain there still, according to the 1932 *True Detective.*

There are over twelve thousand bodies buried in the cemetery today. What makes this cemetery truly unique, however, is its design. The grounds are only a few hundred feet in width but more than a mile in length. There are very few monuments or angel statues but thousands of tombstones, with old and new mixed among each other. The cemetery is still in use today by the living and the dead.

The ghost lights of Elm Lawn are perhaps the most famous of the paranormal activity that inhabits this place of rest. Eyewitnesses have claimed to see glowing balls of light appear from nowhere and float gently through the cemetery, changing directions and then vanishing. Within the paranormal community, there is much debate on the existence of orbs. When these orbs appear in photographs, many experts claim them to be simply dust or moisture particles that are illuminated close to the camera lens. The proximity to the lens makes them appear large in size and producing their own light. On the other hand, some believe them to be the simplest form of spirit energy. Photographs have been captured of orbs without the use of the flash. They have been captured being obscured by objects that can show depth, and, as in Elm Lawn, some orbs have been seen by the naked eye.

In general, Elm Lawn is a very peaceful cemetery, although it is active. Rick Rowe, a paranormal investigator from the Paranormal and Ghost Society, has conducted several investigations in the cemetery. He has seen moving shadow figures with his own eyes. He watched a figure walk from behind a set of trees into an open area of the cemetery. He described it as "having legs and solid black in color. It was definitely moving away from us. As we watched it just vanished. It knew it was being watched." While there on their investigation, members of the team also encountered a glowing red light that moved quickly, materializing in the open and disappearing behind a headstone. Are these the restless spirits of the Shell family who are angered over the movement of their bodies, or is it something more?

FOREST LAWN CEMETERY

1411 Delaware Avenue, Buffalo, New York
www.Forest-Lawn.com

In 1832, the first case of cholera reached Buffalo. The city was seriously affected by the disease. Most of the treatments at the time were experimental because the epidemic was not yet understood. An individual would be in good health in the morning and in his grave by the evening. Death carts would patrol the streets, and when there was an indication of death in the home, the drivers would pound on the door yelling, "Bring out the dead." Bodies were not allowed to remain unburned for more than an hour or two, with the remains being buried shortly afterward. Most of the time, individuals who died were buried the same day of their passing. Cemeteries began to fill quickly, but within the course of a few months the outbreak had ended. Seventeen years later, the second outbreak of cholera occurred. Although not as severe as the first, it took a toll of nine hundred lives, as

Consider where you
ghost hunt before you go;
not all cemeteries have
stories like Forest Lawn.

told in the 2002 *Buffalonian*. This forced the need for a new burial ground far from the city and led to the birth of Forest Lawn.

In 1849, Forest Lawn Cemetery became the city of Buffalo's farthest north burial ground. Charles Clark originally purchased eighty acres of land for the cemetery. Over the years, the farmers who surrounded the cemetery contributed additional land, which now constitutes the over 269 acres that are there today. Some people of note who are laid to rest inside the cemetery include dozens of United States congressmen, writers, explorers and one gentleman named Alfred Southwick. The name may not ring a bell, but his invention will. Southwick was the inventor of the electric chair. By all counts there are more than 152,000 people buried here. Among all of those, there must be a story or two of phantoms that roam the grounds.

Forest Lawn is one of Buffalo's largest and most beautiful cemeteries. It is also one of the most well patrolled by security in Buffalo. One evening, a former security guard recalled driving through the cemetery grounds and coming upon a set of headlights not far ahead of him. This was the second time he had driven through the cemetery that evening, so he was certain no one had gotten locked in accidentally, which can happen in a place this large. As he got closer, the vehicle began to move away. The closer he got to it, the faster the car began to speed up. All the guard could see were the tail lights of an older model dark car. As it rounded one of the corners of the cemetery, it vanished. The phantom car has been sighted many times by many different people in the cemetery and always seems up for a good chase. Maybe it's the spirit of a teenager from the past who used to enjoy drag racing, or perhaps something else.

No cemetery would be complete without its own tale of a "lady in white." Forest Lawn's lady in white is the spirit of a small girl about the age of ten. There have been reports of her chronicled over the past fifty years by visitors and employees of the cemetery. She is often seen wearing a long white evening gown, walking barefoot in the grass. Legend has it that this is the small girl whom people will often see outside the gates on Delaware Avenue. As people pass by, they become concerned that a young girl is out late at night in her nightclothes. When they stop to see if she needs help, she vanishes, according to the 2008 *Buffalo Downtowner.*

GOODLEBERG CEMETERY

Goodleberg Road, South Wales, New York

Goodleberg Cemetery is a burial ground just south of Buffalo in the small town of South Wales, New York. Goodleberg has many secrets within its boundaries that have brought people from miles around, even from other states, to discover its mystery. What has been left in the wake is a small pioneer cemetery that lies in ruin. What are the legends and experiences that people have had, and are they true? Here lies the truth to Goodleberg Cemetery as we have found it.

The legend of Goodleberg began with the sole spirit of a Native American who haunted the area surrounding the cemetery, but in the 1950s the legend became more interesting. The legend spoke of a woman in black who would haunt the area near the now abandoned bridge just south of the cemetery. It was said that a physician had killed her, and if you listened you would hear his hounds howling at her at night. After killing her, he was said to have hanged himself from the large tree inside the cemetery, while other accounts have him being burned alive in his home. The home was at the corner of Goodleberg and Hunter's Creek Roads; some versions say that the stone walls of the cemetery were the actual foundation of his home. Well, in the mid-1980s another facet became part of the legend. It was learned that the physician was an abortion doctor and he threw the aborted fetuses in a small pond just behind the cemetery. There were also legends born about Satanist activity in the area, with rituals involving animal sacrifice. One author suggests that Goodleberg means "hill of ghouls." Goodleberg Cemetery has been a spot for teenagers to gather for the past forty years. Were these legends told to add excitement to a Saturday evening of drinking or fun? Or were the legends true, and is there truly something evil lurking among the tombstones in South Wales, New York?

Several years ago, Western New York Paranormal began a study of the cemetery and the surrounding area. Members of the group began by having some of their researchers collect stories and experiences from visitors, including laypeople and other investigative teams that had visited the site over the past years. They then conducted historical research of the region, combing through newspapers of the area, concentrating on the time period of 1940 to 1960. Their thought was that if such a horrific crime did occur, there must be some evidence of it documented. The

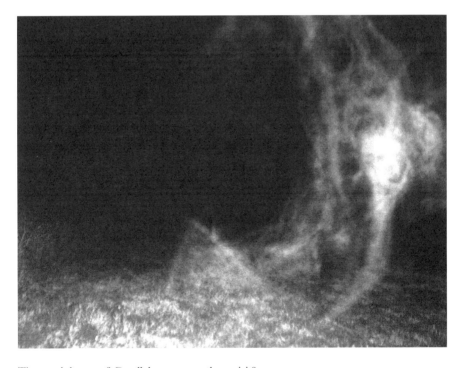

The good doctor of Goodleberg or a restless spirit?

team spoke with local residents about anything they may have observed or experienced and also with historians and local authors. Finally, it sent a fresh team in with little to no knowledge of Goodleberg Cemetery for a paranormal investigation.

It was a warm evening, July 7, 2005. The team members arrived about 11:00 p.m. They were only in the cemetery for about thirty minutes before they started to get activity. The activity wasn't what they had hoped for; it was from the local teenage population. By 12:30 a.m., the cemetery was filled with at least two dozen people coming out for a "scary date," but there were also families with parents and grandparents, and one of the most interesting was a young father bringing his six- and eight-year-olds to show them the "ghosts." The team waited roadside for the crowd to clear and reentered the Goodleberg about 2:00 a.m. A standard investigation was conducted recording EVP, digital photography and video with tri-field meter readings. Of course, orbs were captured, but the team didn't place much credence on them since there can be so many logical explanations for those type of photographic anomalies. About 3:30 a.m., a very interesting photograph was taken just north of the tree line outside the cemetery bounds. It was a mist photograph that showed the existence of several faces attempting to manifest. This was coupled with a dramatic twenty-degree temperature drop and fluctuating tri-field meter readings in that area. Later, a soft EVP was discovered on the digital audio recorder. It was very faint so it was impossible to determine exactly what the words said, but it sounded like, "Where is my baby?" The team also captured moving mist along the roadside with a stationary video camera. It seemed to cross the road. There was nothing else extraordinary about the investigation—no presence of "the doctor," crawling babies or even the famed hell hounds. It didn't live up to the legends of being the most haunted cemetery in western New York.

The research team then compared the reports from people who had visited the site in the past. Interestingly enough, there were only two reports of things happening inside the cemetery. One experience reported inside the cemetery itself was through the use of a Ouija board, and the second involved an interaction with a shadow-like creature that pinned a teenager against a tree by his throat. It was later discovered that the shadow figure was in actuality a local resident dressed all in black trying to scare people away from the cemetery. The remainder of the experiences occurred outside the bounds of the hallowed ground. These experiences usually ranged from handprints on cars to, the most popular, vehicles not starting and flashlights dying. Locals had reports of a horse and carriage, all in black, riding north on the road at dusk and disappearing by the abandoned bridge. There had been no actual experiences involving "the doctor," crawling babies or the hell hounds.

This led the team of Western New York Paranormal to investigate more into the historical aspect of this case for leads. What they found was an interesting buildup to a legend. The legend has its beginnings about 1811, when a young child named Isral Reed was tomahawked and scalped at Black Rock by a local Iroquois hunter. His scalp was used to make a tobacco purse for the hunter, who was later tracked down and hanged from a tree by Isral's brother. The Iroquois hunter was then buried under the tree that was then the property of Isaac Hall—now Goodleberg Cemetery. This is where the legend is born involving the death of children and someone hanging from a tree. The legend didn't reappear until the late 1940s.

In 1949, a woman whom the local newspapers denoted as Mrs. Lindemann came up missing. She resided in Kenmore, New York, and was the wife of a dentist, Dr. Lindemann. She was last seen alive wearing all black. She became known as the woman in black. A few days later, she was found mutilated, with her body parts spread over three different counties. A farmer named Guy Whipple found her torso in his field just off Hunter's Creek Road in South Wales. Not much farther down the road, her mutilated head was discovered. It had been dragged into the road by several dogs and had become their plaything. From conversations with author Mason Winfield, these events seem to fit the time period of when the "doctor's abortions" occurred. Approximately six months passed, and the police had a suspect but no evidence. That is, until they received an anonymous note with a crude sketch of a home that resembled an abandoned one on Hunter's Creek Road. They searched the home but found nothing. One year later, this same house burned down. Police found the owner, whom they believed to be the prime suspect in the grisly murder, inside the remains of the house. He had killed himself by sitting in the middle of his bedroom surrounded by the gasoline-soaked rags that started the fire. Police searched the entire house and drained the pool on the property, but found no hard evidence.

The events surrounding Goodleberg become more intriguing when, in the late 1980s, police were called to the cemetery for the disturbance of several grave sites of children. The bodies were unearthed and the bones found in a nearby field. Time passed and there appeared dead cats on the property, which appeared to have been killed during some ritual. There were reports of rituals being conducted around the area, with pentagram-type circles being discovered. What could all of this mean? Is this all connected? Yes, it is.

Urban legends are much like the story circles children perform in school, where a sentence is whispered from one child to another and by the end of the circle, the sentence is completely different from how it began. Let's follow through these historical reports and compare them to the legend of Dr. "Goodleberg" or Dr. "Speaker."

Let's start off with the hanging figure in the Goodleberg tree. Historical records show this event to have taken place on the land of Isaac Hall, who was an ancestor of the family that currently owns the land around the cemetery. The cemetery first began burials in 1811 and the hanging took place in 1814. This could lend credence to this part of the legend. There does remain the question, however, of why the settlers would kill someone on hallowed ground and bury an Iroquois among the people who hated him for his crime.

The second part of the legend was born in 1949 with the murder of Dr. Linderman's wife and the discovery of her body parts along the road near Goodleberg. This is where the legend comes from of the lady in black who wanders the road in that area searching for her "babies." The idea of babies coming into the legend did not begin until much later, when the grave robbers disturbed the graves of children in the cemetery, leaving bones in a nearby field near a pond. This is where people got the idea of the babies rising up from the water in the pond, but in actuality the pond is an irrigation pond used by a local farm. It was man-made and built approximately ten years earlier. The idea of the walls of Goodleberg being the old foundation of his home is unwarranted since the fire occurred in 1950 and the cemetery has been in use since 1811.

The "abortion doctor" had hell hounds that could be heard at night. The hell hounds were actually born from the newspaper report of dogs dragging Ms. Linderman's head into the road by the corner of Hunter's Creek and Goodleberg Roads. The hounds that visitors hear today on a Goodleberg night could very well be the sounds of the local residents' dogs. The team did some extensive research into the actual existence of this doctor. Review of census records revealed no doctors by the name of Goodleberg or any other of the possible names provided to us from other "researchers." It wasn't until recently that there was a physician living in that area, and he is a dentist who resides most of the time in Florida. The idea of the physician can easily be traced back to the murder of the woman and her husband, Dr. Linderman.

The reports of feline mutilations and "witchcraft" circles can be well founded in the region, but not because of Satanism. In truth, there are no true Satanic cults active in that region, but that is not to say that teenagers playing around did not attempt to conduct some type of rituals there at one time or another. If one is to look at the population by religion in the region, there are a great number of Pagans and Wiccans in the region surrounding South Wales. When data was reviewed surrounding the timing of the appearance of the pentagrams, they corresponded with Wiccan and Pagan holidays that have great rituals associated with them. Pentagrams are associated in many minds to be related to black magick and Satanism, thanks to Hollywood, but this is not always the case. In fact, the pentagram is a symbol of faith and protection similar to the Christian cross, and in ritual ceremonies it is used for protection. It is actually the intention behind the individual practitioner's magick that is what makes the difference. Finally, the proper name for "hill of ghouls" in German would be *Teufeleiberg*, so that doesn't fit either.

The research has been completed in the field, in the history halls and in interviews. So what of the famous Goodleberg Cemetery? The legend of Goodleberg certainly does make a good story for people to hear, but in the opinion of Western New York Paranormal, it is just that—a legend. There is nothing to historically support such legend nor did any paranormal evidence support it. Is the area surrounding Goodleberg Cemetery active

Goose Hill Cemetery.

paranormally? It absolutely is. We collected numerous unexplained phenomenons in the areas *surrounding* the cemetery—in the fields and on the road—there are spirits there among you.

GOOSE HILL CEMETERY

Centerline Road, Sheldon, New York

A nineteenth-century graveyard lies hidden along Centerline Road. Once known as Goose Hill after a local farmer who once raised geese there, this place of rest is now formally known as St. John's Cemetery. The small cemetery has about forty stones in it, with many of them weathered away by the elements or broken in half as a result of time. The locals tell of the cemetery being very active though not by visitors, but by the residents of the cemetery.

The local stories of Goose Hill Cemetery tell of shadows that run through the woods and whispers in the darkness. What makes these whispers different from other locations is the language that they speak in: German. A majority of the residents who rest in this burial place were of German descent, as can be seen by the inscriptions in German on the headstones. Paranormal teams have reported strange glowing balls of light visible with the naked eye, sounds of footsteps in the grass and physical touches.

DEATHLY INSANE

Through the history of New York State, asylums have had a long, torrid role. Most of these now abandoned buildings began as poorhouses that transformed into lunatic asylums, wards when epidemics broke out and even orphanages. Many times they would serve multiple purposes at the same time. They were places of filth, torment and cruelty. It is no wonder that the spirits that remain are often confused, deranged and sometimes even inhuman.

BUFFALO PSYCHIATRIC CENTER

400 Forest Avenue, Buffalo, New York

In 1869, a bright Buffalo physician by the name of Dr. James White proposed to the state legislator that an asylum be built within the city limits of Buffalo. His idea was the origin of what is now the beautiful Buffalo Psychiatric Center. The State Hospital Organization was established in 1869, and in 1871 it chose Henry Hobson Richardson to be the architect on the job. By looking at the massive structure today, stretching across most of Forest Avenue, you can see they made a wise choice. Workers began breaking ground for what was originally called Buffalo State Asylum for the Insane in June 1871, though it wasn't until November 18, 1889, that the hospital started to accept patients. It actually took until 1895 to complete this beautiful structure. Though Henry Hobson Richardson died in 1886, his plans were carried out and this massive structure was completed. The layout of the asylum consisted of the center administration building with two breathtaking towers, expanded by five connected but separate ward buildings. The outside of the building was covered in brown sandstone and red brick. The interior of the building was very elegant, and the buildings all

Buffalo Psychiatric Center.

were lavish in beauty. In the late 1800s, it was, and still is today, one of the most beautiful structures the country has ever seen.

The beauty of the building may be the only pleasant memory of this hospital. It is rumored that patients were subjected to cruel treatments. It has also been said that there were, and still exist today, catacombs underneath the physicality that still hold many of the unorthodox equipment used on the patients, though due to the inability to enter the building, this may just be hearsay. As time went by, the building started to show its age. In 1969, three wards on the eastern side of the facility were torn down. In 1973, the Buffalo State Asylum for the Insane was placed in the National Historic Landmark List. In 1974, the seven remaining wards were put out of use. In 1994, the hospital administration building was finally closed down permanently.

Many mysteries surround this deteriorating gem, including the famous mystery of Sadie Mcmullin. This strange tale began in the year 1890, when the young Sadie Mcmullin threw little Delia Brown, age six, and Nellie May Conners, age eight, off a railroad bridge over Murder Creek in Akron, New York. In a panic, the villagers searched everywhere for the missing girls, not knowing the terrors they had endured. About three o'clock in the morning, they found the body of Nellie, who had perished in the river. They also found Delia, who was still alive. When she was found, she told the villagers in a sarcastic comment, even for an eight-year-old, that Sadie Mcmullin was the one who had committed this terrible crime. Sadie was brought to trial, and at the end of the trial she was acquitted and committed to the Buffalo State Asylum for the Insane for two years. While in Buffalo she was treated for epilepsy. According to her nephew, Mark Saglian, after her release, she vanished and was never seen or heard from again. He also, in searching for the past of this missing aunt, found the statement that she wrote in custody of the police, admitting to the whole crime.

Sadie was among many of the over fifty thousand patients to see the walls of this structure. When the building was opened and there was an abundance of patients that needed care, at some points over two thousand patients were living in the wards that were designed to hold only six hundred. As we look back in time, the treatments for these unfortunate patients were absolutely terror-filled and cruel; however, on the other hand, it is also said that the asylum became a refuge for many. This is why the Buffalo Psychiatric Center is still a busy place. Many of the patients who endured the terrors of the treatments and saw the asylum as a sanctuary are still said to walk the halls, even today.

In the 1950s, hospital workers began the use of a new tranquilizing medication that helped ease many of the symptoms of the ailments that the patients had. As the 1960s began, the treatment of the patients began to change. Workers began to treat the patients in a less restrictive form of treatment. The Community of Mental Health Act of 1963 was then passed, allowing for care outside of state facilities, and out-care treatment became very popular. With all the breakthroughs in medication, institutions like Buffalo became less and less needed. Throughout the years, medical procedure did have many breakthroughs, and compassion became part of the job, though for some it was far too late for that.

A young man named David Heglund recalls walking down the street that runs in front of the asylum one summer. According to Heglund, the energy that surrounds the building itself feels "thick and muddy like walking through quicksand." As he was walking down the sidewalk with his partner, Heglund came across an older gentleman walking a small white dog. Oddly, the elderly gentleman stopped for a moment when he came to the two gentlemen. He turned to them and then pointed to the building. He said, "Terrible things happen inside that building. If you listen, you can sometimes hear the screams coming from inside." He then turned and continued down the sidewalk with his dog. Thinking this was very odd, Heglund turned to look again at the gentleman they had just encountered, but he had vanished. There was no sign that he had ever been there.

The Buffalo Psychiatric Center sits directly across the street from the Buffalo State College dorms. Many of the students there recall many instances of looking out across the street to see lights on in the two towers. This is quite strange, since the building has been vacant for many years. It has also been rumored around the campus that screams and crying have been heard from inside the walls. In an interview with a man who chose not to be named, he told me that when he was sixteen years old, when the seven wards had been shut down, he and a friend snuck into the abandoned parts of the building. They said that the basement looked like cells for a jail, with only small holes through which to pass food and water. They didn't last very long in there, as the sounds of screaming and banging scared them out, running, not looking back. Psychics who have walked the properties have often become disoriented, leaving with the feeling of sadness and shedding tears as they drive away.

College students today often joke about times when they have been inside the building and the beauty and history that is going to waste. One student laughed and said, "It's weird, there are leaves all over in the main corridor, but no broken windows?!" I must say, if you are a thrill-seeker, this building is not one to tamper with. The age and deterioration have taken their toll

Even this cross doesn't help the dead to rest at the psychiatric center.

on the building. It is very unsafe to try to go in alone. This beautiful empty building is highly guarded by the Buffalo Police Department and has a heavy fence surrounding the whole property. Though you are more than welcome to view this beautiful piece of history, you need to do it from outside of the fence line. A large rock sits quietly outside of the fence, right in the center of the cement walkway that used to run to the main entrance. On the rock is a plaque noting its historic relevance. Today, the Richardson Olmsted Cooperation is busy at work trying to find alternate uses for this beautiful structure. Uses discussed have included everything from condominiums or hotels to an expansion of the Buffalo State College.

GENESEE COUNTY ASYLUM

11001 Bethany Center Road, East Bethany, New York

The Genesee County Asylum, located approximately one hour southwest of Buffalo, is an enigma in the world of the paranormal. It can easily be compared to other public haunts, such as the Moundsville Penitentiary in West Virginia, the Mansfield State Reformatory in Ohio and even the Stanley Hotel in Colorado. Historical records show that the property was an old stagecoach stop before it was purchased in 1826 by Genesee County, which then opened it as a poorhouse. Throughout the nineteenth century, the location served as an asylum for the insane as well as an orphanage. By the 1940s, the property had become a nursing home. It was finally closed down in 1974, according to a 2007 edition of *Ghost!* magazine.

There is a lot of mystery and legend that surrounds this property and building. In fact, while the building was operating as an asylum and orphanage, rumors ran rampant that a coven of witches operated within the walls of the institution. Not all witches are bad; many are just misunderstood. These individuals, however, reportedly worshiped the dark arts, and there were suggestions made by many of the locals of that time that rituals, including magick and infant sacrifice, were held within the building itself. Many of these events occurred on the fourth floor of the building, where the nurses had their living quarters. The allegations of witchcraft and sacrifice cannot be substantiated; however, when the building was undergoing some repair on the fourth floor, a local worker discovered a ring hidden within the walls. This ring was silver and had the face of a horned creature on it—a common symbol of demonic worship. It was discovered in the room where the head nurse resided.

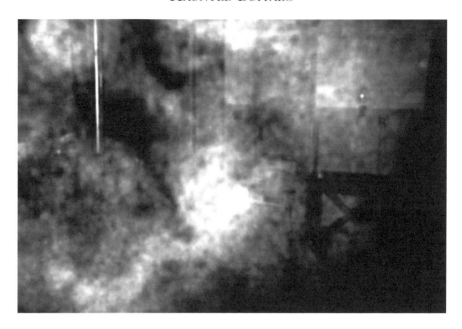

All who wander are not lost.

Through the decades, rumors of hauntings continued to circulate regarding this building and its property. Teenagers would break into the building to try to scare one another, some even performing rituals on the top floor. Passersby would see an older woman sitting in an old wicker wheelchair in one of the overlooks. She would just smile and wave as cars would pass by. Individuals entering the building would hear strange noises, doors closing and chairs moving around by themselves—all without explanation.

In 2004, one of the first paranormal investigation teams entered the building. The Paranormal and Ghost Society, a Buffalo-based organization, brought investigators armed with cameras to see what mysteries they could unlock from within the walls of the building. Interestingly enough, they were the first group to capture photographs of mist and ectoplasm at the building. As time went on, other groups began to come and investigate as well.

In 2005, Western New York Paranormal began its initial investigations of the property. One evening, the organization had planned a brief meeting on-site to discuss group business. During the meeting, one of the investigators, Bill, kept looking over into the darkness. Quietly, he said, "They're not happy we're here." Yet the meeting continued. At the end, Bill was heading toward the stairwell. He was determined to get to the fourth floor. As he reached the stairwell, he turned to other investigators and said, "They're killing them. I have to do something!" and began to climb the stairs. His eyes had a look unlike anything that any of the investigators had ever seen before. It was a blank look with nothing behind the eyes.

One of the investigators grabbed Bill's hand, stopping him from climbing the stairs, and explained that it was important for Bill to leave the building and ground himself, but Bill was intent. Several other members of the organization heard the commotion and came to help. They led Bill back down the stairs and toward the main doors. As he was going down the stairs, one of the investigators stopped in his tracks, turned to look behind him up the stairs and then began praying in Hebrew as the others took Bill outside of the building.

In the parking lot, Bill seemed to calm back down and relax. After taking a few deep breaths, he seemed fine. Since the excitement seemed over, one investigator who had a tape recorder on him went into the building to grab some additional equipment that had been left in there. As he did, he approached another researcher and made the comment that he thought Bill had just been possessed. Suddenly, the main door burst open again. Bill was hastily coming through the doorway, heading straight back toward the stairwell with a number of individuals following him. Three men grabbed him, forcing him down into a chair.

"You need to relax, Bill," one of the investigators said. Bill responded, "There is no Bill here. Only Thomas. And you will let me go before I put you in the grave." Holding Bill down, members of the group began to pray; over and over again they said the Lord's Prayer. One individual began commanding the entity to leave in the name of Christ, only to be responded to with vulgarities. Soon he was approached by a pair of Pagans who had come to the meeting that evening. One of them, with crystals in hand, came to Bill while channeling her spirit guide. She commanded that Thomas leave him. The spirit had no right to the body. It had no choice but to leave. After some time, the spirit left and Bill was taken home.

This sounds like the storyline of a horror movie, but it happened. It was captured on audio and on video. When investigators went back and reviewed the audio, they found a bone-chilling EVP. When the investigator made the comment that he thought Bill had been possessed, there was a response on the tape. It was a low, gravelly, inhuman, serpentine-sounding voice saying, "Yessssssssssss." As the Pagans demanded that the entity leave, video recording was going on, and as the entity left, a visible spirit orb was witnessed rising up out of Bill.

Although there are fear-filled stories that have occurred at Genesee County Asylum, there have also been some very touching stories. In one

The mist of a spirit. *Photograph by Nora Ballard.*

of the first public ghost hunts, a woman had come in with the hopes of contacting a family member who had long since passed there. She explained that her grandmother had once been a patient at the nursing home and had died after suffering a fall in one of the stairways.

It was early in the night when she made it down to where the cafeteria once was, and she was feeling a bit disappointed that she hadn't seen any signs of her grandmother. She had experienced odd feelings in different places but found nothing she could really validate. One of the investigator/guides was in the cafeteria at that time and walked over to her with a compass in hand. He explained to her how sometimes spirits can be found using compasses. The fact that spirits are energy allows them to manipulate magnetic fields, and sometimes an individual standing completely still can experience the compass of a needle moving back and forth by as much as 5 or 10 degrees. Usually that means that there is paranormal activity in the area. Being a bit of a skeptic, she took the compass in hand and asked the question out loud, "Are you here, Grandma?" She looked down, and as she did, the compass began to move. It didn't move just five or ten degrees; it spun completely around several times, 360 degrees, and the woman began to cry. "Grandma," she said. She used that compass to find the place in the building where her grandmother had died and then placed a single rose at the spot. "Grandma, go to God now," she said. Her trip to the building had been complete.

GHOSTS AT WORK

It is said that when a person dies, he goes to the place that influenced him the most in life. This could be a place where he spent a lot of time or possibly could be a place where something tragic happened to him. There are many spirits that continue to return to these places as either a residual energy (just repeat an action or event over and over again) or as an intelligent entity (knowing all that goes on around it). In the city of Buffalo, even haunted places go far beyond homes, museums and landmarks…they include places where people work every day.

BUFFALO CITY HALL

222 City Hall, Buffalo, New York
www.ci.buffalo.ny.us

Three brothers—Israel, Nelson and Isaac—marched down the street from the old courthouse to Niagara Square. Each of the brothers was shrouded with a white hood over his face, and they were preceded by three coffins, one for each of the brothers to be buried in after their execution. The brothers had been convicted of the 1824 murder of John Love, a local farmer who had apparently been murdered over a small amount of money. He disappeared in June 1824 and was found a few months later in a shallow grave at the back of his own property. As they walked down the street, more than thirty thousand people gathered to watch the hanging execution of the three brothers. A band played a slow death march while the surrounding crowd just observed, as reported in the February 4, 2007 edition of the *Buffalo News*. As they reached the wooden gallows that were built not far from where city hall stands, Israel let out a loud, high-pitched miserable wail. His brothers

Buffalo City Hall, where sounds of dying men can still be heard.

followed, and then the crowd began. The sound was traditionally made during the mourning of an Irishman. The keening can still be heard today.

CENTRAL TERMINAL

495 Paderewski Drive, Buffalo, New York
www.BuffaloCentralTerminal.org

In 1848, Buffalo saw its first rail terminal on Exchange Street. It was a relatively small brick building that would serve the flow of passengers through downtown Buffalo. Less than forty years later, Buffalo had become a bustling hub of commerce for those traveling to and from the western portion of the United States. In an effort to capitalize on the flow of people through the region, community leaders proposed a "union station" in 1889. It would be one centralized location for all passenger trains to come in and out of the city, providing for easier transportation and commerce. The plan didn't go through until 1925, but until that time several rail companies shared locations at the Exchange Street site.

The New York Central Railroad signed an agreement in 1925 to build a grand central terminal at its current location just two and a half miles from downtown Buffalo. The construction of the seventeen-story terminal took two years to complete. On Saturday, June 22, 1929, the terminal opened to the public with an elegant gala for more than two thousand guests who watched the first train depart at 2:10 p.m. The terminal had more than two hundred trains arrive daily in its height. It could not foresee the trouble ahead with the coming of the Great Depression.

The Great Depression caused the New York Central Railroad to lose more than 50 percent of its operating revenue and more than 80 percent of its net revenue from passengers between 1929 and 1933. This was devastating for Buffalo's new central terminal. It became quickly apparent that the terminal far exceeded the current and future needs of the railways. The governmental support of the railway transportation system declined. Soon the maintenance and repairs of the rail systems were falling entirely upon the railroad companies, while the government began to subsidize other areas of transportation, such as the automotive industry, busing and airlines. The tremendous amount of taxes being paid by the terminal was going to aid the competition. In less than five years, the terminal became obsolete. By the mid-1930s, the New York Central Railroad had downgraded much of its facilities and closed off many sections of the building due to the decline in passenger travel.

As World War II grew closer, the rail industry became a major component in transportation. The railway systems began to transport manufactured goods, raw materials for military production and passengers. They carried 91 percent of the military goods for the nation and 95 percent of the military personnel. The hostilities of the war caused shortages in gasoline and oil, which also forced civilian travelers to utilize other forms of transportation. The rail industry became overwhelmed and worked as quickly as it could to keep up with the demand, many times putting its oldest passenger cars into use. Gone were the days of Art Deco transportation. This caused many consumers to swear never to use rail transportation again once the war was over.

After the war, the railroads thought that they could bring their passengers back with faster and more elegant trains. This never happened. The American

An aerial view of the terminal when it was built. *Courtesy of the Library of Congress.*

A vintage view. *Courtesy of the Library of Congress.*

population had its cars back and became enchanted with the airline industry, which could get them to their destination much faster than any rail. The passenger railway industry continued its decline. The 1950s experienced a host of consolidation in the rail industry. In 1957, the New York Central Railroad lost over $110,000 on the central terminal. All that remained was some local service and five daily trains to Niagara Falls. In 1959, the Public Transportation Commission allowed the railroad to terminate those services to Niagara Falls. By 1961, only one train ran daily through the terminal from Buffalo to New York City. On December 3, 1967, the last run was made from the terminal.

The years to follow saw several different owners of the terminal. For a short time, the Penn Central System attempted to operate a rail terminal from the location, followed by Amtrak. In 1979, the terminal was placed up for auction with only one bidder, Anthony Fedele. He purchased the terminal for the sum of $75,000. He planned on turning the terminal into a hotel and events center, but those plans never came about. Buffalo was changing. The area of the city where the terminal was located was quickly becoming the "bad section." Fedele encountered this firsthand when he attempted to bring tenants into the building. It seems that the only tenant he was able to secure was himself; he resided on the third floor of the terminal. In 1980, the terminal experienced a short-lived boom when a movie company decided to use it for a major motion picture, *Best Friends*, starring Goldie Hawn and Burt Reynolds. The location was perfect; the terminal looked as it had in its heyday. In 1983, the building was about to be pulled out from underneath Fedele in light of over $140,000 owed in back taxes. He made concessions with the city by paying approximately $10,000 and agreeing to pay $2,000 per month until the debt was settled. In 1984, the terminal was listed on the National Register of Historical Landmarks, and as a result, Fedele was relieved of the remaining back taxes. In the late 1980s, a fire destroyed the third floor of the building where Fedele's apartment was located. He gave up ownership in 1986.

The building was now abandoned and left wide open for vandalism. By the 1990s, over 75 percent of the terminal had been pillaged. Artifacts were removed, pieces of architecture taken and sold at auction and anything made of copper removed and sold. There was even a brass statue that stood in the terminal that was destroyed when a former owner backed into it with his truck so that he could remove a chandelier. The statue lay in pieces. Devastation came from not only the human force but also nature. The elements began to erode the building. Water fell through the roof and into the cracks of the building. During the winter, the water would freeze,

Buffalo Central Terminal as it stands today.

destroying more of the architecture. In the basement, a water main broke, and being unable to reach it to fix it, the water authority left it alone. The problem was that water expands when it freezes. As it did this each winter, it weakened the foundation of the building more and more. The tower of the building was littered with more than thirty years' of railway paperwork and broken windows and doors. It became a very dangerous place to be around. One city worker stated that, while walking through the main terminal area, anyone would "need to wear a hard hat and a rain jacket because it was like walking through Niagara Falls."

The terminal was purchased in 1997 by the Central Terminal Preservation Company. It has pledged to secure the building and to stop the destruction of this unique piece of Buffalo's history. Since the restoration project began, activity has increased again at the terminal. Volunteers are in and out day after day cleaning and rebuilding, but passengers from the past are also making their presence known. According to Tracy Dolan, a member of the Central Terminal Preservation Company, there have been many reports of unexplained figures in the building. She recalls one day watching two men walking over to a drinking fountain in the main terminal area. They bent over, took a drink and then disappeared. The men not only vanished but the fountain did as well. All that remained in the area was a hole in the wall where the fountain had once been.

A female apparition has also been seen wandering the main terminal area, with cold spots appearing, even on the warmest of days. Restoration volunteer Adam Vester heard a disembodied voice ask him in German, "Vestor, was Sie ist, hier tuend?" The translation in English is, "What are you doing here?" Why would a voice come through in German? What many people don't realize is that German prisoners of war were brought to do maintenance work on the building during World War II. Other volunteers have watched figures walk past them in the main terminal, only to turn to see that they were not really there. The main terminal area isn't the only place where there seems to be activity. The third floor, which was once the apartment of Anthony Fedele, also has a unique energy all its own. People have claimed to hear voices and footsteps there. Some have claimed to see a dark, shadowy figure moving about the floor. When it is approached, it disappears around a corner.

The Atlantic Paranormal Society (TAPS) investigated Buffalo's Central Terminal as part of the Sci Fi Channel's television program *Ghost Hunters*. The group found the building to contain some extremely active paranormal phenomena. On the main floor in the terminal area, cameras were set up along with audio recorders surrounding the area where the two apparitions were sighted at the drinking fountain. Although they didn't capture evidence of their existence, members of the team did hear what sounded like a woman's laughter and footsteps down the concourse. On the third floor, in Fedele's old apartment, the team began to conduct EVP work and used thermal imaging. One of the investigators assured the spirits that they were not there to hurt them, and a response came back that sounded like a voice. It then came again, followed by a bang. Team members heard the sounds with their own ears, and it was also captured on the audio equipment. The camcorder they were using on that floor mysteriously shut itself off in their hands, even though there was battery life left with plenty of time left on the tape. After reviewing the thermal footage from a separate camera, they found an unexplained heat signature on the third floor. A possible spirit?

In the main concourse area, team members were able to use K2 meters as spiritual communication devices to ask questions. They set up responses with the spirits—blinking once for yes and twice for no. As they were questioning the spirit, one of the investigators noticed that there was a shadow blocking one of the windows. He asked the spirit to come closer, and as he did, the K2 meter reacted. By the end of their questioning, they were able to determine that the spirit was indeed a female from the 1940s, the same woman whom they heard laughing earlier and whom others had seen walking in the concourse.

It would seem that the Buffalo Central Terminal is as busy now as it was over fifty years ago.

OLD BUICK DEALERSHIP

Hamburg, New York

Sitting quietly in the town of Hamburg is a building that is still in use today, though now it is used for a cooperation-owned after-market repair service that wishes to remain anonymous. This building was built in the early 1920s as one of the most elegant and elaborate Buick dealerships in the state of New York. In fact, it was one of the first Buick dealerships in the state. The original three-story structure still remains complete with a showroom, a repair shop and vehicle bays, with three massive warehouses off the back. The upper portion of the building was mainly offices. In the heyday of the dealership, it was said that many parties were held at the dealership and the third floor was the place to be. The second floor had showers and locker rooms for the employees.

Today, if you talk to the employees of this business, they will all tell you tales of supernatural activity that they have had to endure over the years. Many mechanics have told of tires rolling off top shelves and hitting them. Other workers have complained of having an eerie feeling in certain parts of the building. Many of the workers will not even venture into the unused second and third floors due to fear. Workers have often heard voices talking with one another when no one else is present in the building. The smell of cigarette smoke has also been noted throughout the building. When a psychic was brought onto the property, she noted that there were three different entities in the building. When she explained the appearance of one of them, it matched that of a previous owner.

Even today, you can walk through the upper warehouse and still see the elaborate lit-up signs from the earlier days of the building sitting against the walls of this massive empty room. Though all of the second and third floors are not in use today, they are still busy with activity from the other side.

SHANNON ENTERPRISE

75 Main Street, North Tonawanda, New York

Stories of the spirits that roam the buildings of Shannon Enterprise stretch far back in the local lore of North Tonawanda. Locals can remember the sales personnel and mechanics of the former Keyser Cadillac dealership, which was the building's first tenant, sharing their encounters with the ghostly presence there. The employees assured others that the spirits that roam there were not malicioius, but they were pranksters. Their phantom antics still continue today inside the building.

Shannon Enterprise operates two very unique and separate manufacturing businesses from this haunted location. One facet of the business is the production of custom-fit, reusable and removable blanket insulation. The specific type of insulation is designed for use in insulating machinery and piping. The other portion of the business involves the production of Corian countertops for use in the housing industry. No matter what is sold or manufactured at the location, it doesn't seem to change the presence of the paranormal here. Employees have shared with customers that machinery turns on and off by itself, lights flicker and turn on for no reason and there have been sightings of a male figure that walks the building in the night.

In order to either prove or disprove the claims of the paranormal, Shannon Enterprise invited Niagara Falls Paranormal to its manufacturing facility to conduct an investigation. In preparation for the investigation, the management shut down all of the equipment for the evening. There would be no extraneous noise and no way that any of the manufacturing equipment could create false readings on the investigators' meters. In one of the rooms that was reported to have a lot of activity, an investigator sat in the dark attempting to record EVPs. As he worked through his session, there was a sudden loud hissing noise that sounded like one of the machines turning itself on. The sound continued to hiss through the silence for about thirty seconds and scared the investigator. The manager was brought into the room and asked to start one of the machines up. As he did, the investigator stated that the sound heard was nothing like what he had experienced and captured on tape.

As the evening went on, the paranormal experiences continued. As two investigators were walking through the office section of the building, they came across an office that caught their attention. Inside the room there seemed to be a light source that was turning on and off. It was as if someone was turning a desk lamp on and off. This section of the building was supposed to be empty so, curious, the investigators knocked at the door to see who was there. No one answered their knock. They tried the doorknob but the door was locked. One of the investigators went for the manager of the building, who came and unlocked the door. As they entered the room, they found that it was empty. The manager shared that what they had witnessed was a common occurrence reported from that particular office. The entire event was captured on a video recording, but when investigators went back to review the footage, although they captured their reactions to the event, the camera did not capture the light source.

No one knows for certain who the spirits are that haunt this building in North Tonawanda. One thing is for certain: they are dedicated to their work, working late into the night and continuing to work even beyond death.

HISTORIC HAUNTS

Places of great history are often brimming with stories and legends. The Buffalo and Niagara area served as a passageway between the eastern and western sections of the United States. Great numbers of people passed through this place, leaving residual energies behind that can often create imprints of events that last for centuries. There was also much bloodshed on the land, leaving some very unsettled spirits to remind us of these historic atrocities.

DEVIL'S HOLE

New York State Park, Niagara Falls, New York
http://nysparks.state.ny.us/parks/info.asp?parkID=28

Devil's Hole has long had a history of being a place saturated with evil spirits. The Native Americans referred to the cave near Devil's Hole as home to the "Evil One." In Native American mythology, the Evil One was a demonlike snake that was the source of all that was malevolent. Even today, this twenty-six-foot-deep cave is the source of unexplainable moans and screams coming from the darkness. Legends tell of a tribe that once entered the cave, of whom not all returned from the journey. Young braves who entered with dark black hair left with white hair, unable to tell of their encounter because they had lost their minds. The local tribe had such fear of Devil's Hole that in 1689 they warned French explorer Sieur de La Salle to avoid the area. He didn't heed their warning and was murdered by his own men several days after passing the cave.

In 1763, the Seneca Nation attacked a supply wagon coming through the region. During this ambush, dozens of soldiers lost their lives. The bodies,

The place of ancient evil. *Photograph by Eric Muth.*

along with those of the oxen and horses, were driven off the ledge into Devil's Hole; this became known as the Devil's Hole Massacre. It was much later, in 1901, when President William McKinley was assassinated only hours after passing over the area on the Great Gorge Trolley. In 1917, the Great Gorge Trolley lost one of its cars just as it passed over Devil's Hole, plummeting fifty passengers to their deaths. Since that time, countless people have died at the hands of Devil's Hole, in addition to people falling or jumping every year.

FRONTIER HOUSE

Main Street, Lewiston, New York

The Frontier House was once recognized as one of the most prized hotels in western New York. It was a stagecoach stop that saw hundreds of passengers day in and day out as they passed through the region. One of the most famous of the visitors to the Frontier House was a Mason named William Morgan. Morgan was accused by his fellow Masons of preparing to publish the secret rites and rituals of the organization. According to some historical records, Morgan was kidnapped in Canandaguia, New York, and brought to the Frontier House. At the Frontier House, it is said that he changed coaches and continued on his journey to Fort Niagara, but he never arrived there. The stagecoach that Morgan originally arrived in was parked behind the building, and for many years it was never touched. The locals feared that if they disturbed the coach, they too could become implicated in the mysterious disappearance of Morgan. The coach eventually rotted away and disappeared. The original family who built the Frontier House maintained it for a number of years and eventually turned it into a private residence, but not before people such as Mark Twain and President McKinley passed through its doors.

George Rictor purchased the home and added the Frontier House restaurant to the building. In the 1960s, Niagara Falls welcomed more than eleven thousand new laborers to the region, and the rooms began being rented in eight-hour shifts, sleeping three to a room to accommodate the lack of housing. In 1964, James Russell purchased the building and turned the home into a museum with a restaurant. A dining room was added on floor level and a ballroom on the second floor. A Victorian bedroom and early American parlor were also added on the third floor, with a private residence on the forth level. In the early 1970s, a fire devastated much of the building. In 1975, McDonald's Corporation leased the building and renovated it. The company removed the name plaques of all its famous guests to replace it with the famous golden arches.

There are many stories that flow from the Frontier House. One legend explains that in the the construction of the Frontier House, a worker fell from the top of the building and died. His fellow workers buried him in one of the walls. Another legend tells of a Mason who opposed the entire William Morgan affair. Some believe that Morgan was held against his will behind the Frontier House prior to his departure for Fort Niagara. There, of course, is no documented history to support either of these legends; however, this does not mean that the Frontier House does not have spirits from its past still lingering.

Construction workers tell stories of how when they renovated the lower areas of the building into the McDonald's restaurant, their tools would vanish right in front of their eyes. Hammers would be there one minute and then gone the next. Doors and windows would open and close themselves. They also reported hearing strange noises and voices, while another told of seeing the figure of an older gentleman vanish in front of his eyes. An investigator from Niagara Falls Paranormal recalls one evening when he and a friend stopped by the Frontier House shorty after the building had burned down. He remembered that the windows had been broken and everything inside was in a turmoil. As he looked through one of the broken windows, he watched a woman walk down the staircase inside, and he thought to himself how odd it was. She was dressed in a white nightgown. Then he realized that she wasn't completely there; as she walked around the side of the stairs, he could see through her. As he turned to his friend, she vanished without a trace. The ghostly woman in white is perhaps still waiting for her stagecoach to arrive.

IRON ISLAND MUSEUM

998 Lovejoy Street, Buffalo, New York
www.IronIslandMuseum.com

In Buffalo, there is a small community known as Lovejoy. This small area was once owned in part by Millard Fillmore until about 1850. It was then that he sold this piece of land to a neighboring farm owned by the Churchyard family, who farmed the land for over twenty years. In 1877, they deeded the property to the City of Buffalo, which then divided it into smaller building parcels. The population of Lovejoy began to grow quickly as houses began to spring up. Employment in the local grain mills brought immigrant families from Germany, Ireland, Italy and Russia. As the communities expanded, so did the places of worship. In just the small community of Lovejoy, there were ten active churches, each one serving a different ethnic population. One group purchased a small parcel of land where they constructed a simple wooden church. The year was 1888, and Lovejoy now had its first Methodist Episcopal church. In seven short years, the wooden structure grew and changed. The wood was changed to brick and stone and the congregation grew. The church remained an active part of the community until about 1948. Legend has it that an assistant pastor at St. Agnes Church gave the area the unique designation after hearing a train whistle. Recognizing that railroad tracks circled the entire perimeter of the neighborhood, he began to refer to it as Iron Island.

Just two years after the closing of the church, another owner took possession of the property and converted it into a funeral home. He built over some of the structures of the church itself, making it into a more contemporary building fit for its use. The funeral home remained in use until 2001, when it was purchased by Anthony Amigod, who donated the building to the

Iron Island, a place
for the living and the
dead.

Iron Island Preservation Society of Lovejoy. Today, the building is used as
a museum to preserve the historical integrity of the community. It not only
holds memorabilia from the community, but it also seems to have held on to
kindred spirits from the area's past.

Museum owner Linda Hastreiter explains that there are many different
rooms inside the building dedicated to different eras in the history of
the community. One of the first rooms that a visitor to the museum will
encounter is what they call the railroad room. The railroad room contains
artifacts from the rail history of the area, along with some phantoms
from the past. Employees often refer to this area as the children's room. A
glance at the corner of the room will make obvious the reason, as there is
a small pile of toys there for the phantom residents. One of the original
investigation groups at Iron Island was the Toronto Ghost Hunters. Its
members brought with them two psychics in addition to their scientific
equipment. Both psychics felt the presence of a young boy named Tommy
in this particular room. He was between the ages of six and eight. Not
knowing what she believed, Hastreiter went through some of the old files
from the funeral director. In them she discovered that what is now the
railroad room was in the past the viewing room. As she continued to review
the files, she discovered that there was an eight-year-old boy who was
waked from the building in 1958 by the name of Tommy Philangelo. From
that time on, museum workers began to call that spirit Tommy. A few years
later, the Sci Fi Channel's *Ghost Hunters* came to the museum to conduct
an investigation. Shortly after the airing of the episode, a gentleman by
the name of Domanic Philangelo came to the museum. He shared how

he loved the show and explained that he was Tommy's cousin, bringing photographs of Tommy and his sister. One piece of the evidence captured during the show was a simple EVP from the room that said "boat" in a little boy's voice. Domanic explained that Tommy had gone fishing the day before his death with his father down by Lily Dale, New York.

There is also a room in the museum known as the military room. On display are artifacts from various wars that were fought throughout the region and of wars that local residents would have fought in. In this room, visitors have recorded EVPs that sounded like mortar and gunfire. There have been reports of the sound of footsteps walking across the floor of the room in heavy boots. A woman who experienced a specter, who wishes to remain anonymous, reported that she only saw half of a soldier from the waist down. There are many spirits that wander the rooms of Iron Island. Some spirits are brought here by items displayed in the building, while others are remnants of its past.

LOCKPORT CAVES

2 Pine Street, Lockport, New York
www.LockportCave.com

One of the most noteworthy attractions in the Niagara Frontier is the Lockport Caves, though a little-known fact is that there are actually two cave systems that are buried beneath the city. One is a naturally occurring system that was once believed to be able to accommodate a population of 200,000 people, and the other is a hydraulic waterway created by Birdsall Holley. Although the naturally occurring system still exists underneath the city, it has not been easily accessible to the public since 1863, when the Lockport Cave Company began exploration of the cave for potential tourism use. It ran electric lighting through a majority of the cavern system, but the lights generated heat, and the increase in temperature increased the water level in the cave, causing things to melt throughout the spring-fed caves. When combined with heavy spring rains, a great portion of the system filled with silt, filling many access points. The mouth was approximately one hundred feet off where Cave Street is located today. Occasionally, small holes are poked into the cavern system during construction to the area. The last time this happened was in the process of building the police station in Lockport. Reports state that a construction worker supposedly created a small hole in the cavern system, but it was not large enough for anyone to enter. The stories of this cavern system continue today, ranging from its use as a hideout for outlaws to subterranean hideaways for slaves along the Underground Railroad. For now, the system remains an unexplored mystery of the city that lies buried.

In 1832, a local industrialist named Birdsall Holley began to draw industry into the city of Lockport as a result of an engineering marvel he had accomplished. Up until this time, industry had relied on Niagara Falls for much of its hydroelectric power. He envisioned another solution and began construction of a sixteen-hundred-foot hydraulic cave that would run underneath the city. Workers toiled for eighteen-hour days just to gain a few feet through the solid bedrock, at the cost of at least one hundred lives, according to a 2009 interview with Steve Salatino. Once completed, the causeway provided mechanical power for the Holley Manufacturing Company, Lockport Pulp and the United Indurated Fibre Company. The hydraulic cave remained in operatin until 1941, when the pulp plant closed.

Today, the former hydraulic cave operates as the Lockport Cave and Underground Boat Ride. Thousands of tourists visit this attraction every year to experience the history. When you walk in to purchase your ticket for the attraction, you enter into the former city hall building. Psychic Steve Salatino remembers the first time he visited the attraction. "The company I worked for had brought us there as part of a team-building exercise. I can remember when I first walked into the city hall to get my ticket there was a heavy feeling. It wasn't bad, just a feeling of heavy energy and a lot of it," said Salatino. Psychics will often experience sensations of heaviness in areas of high paranormal activity. These can exhibit themselves as tightness in the chest, difficulty breathing or just the sensation as if they were walking through quicksand. "I asked the manager on duty if the caves were haunted and he replied, 'If you want them to be,'" said Salatino. Salatino went on to explain that he was a psychic and paranormal investigator. He was curious whether anyone had ever had any unexplained experiences in the cavern. The manager simply pointed to a bulletin board on the wall and told Salatino to look at the picture of a section of the cavern with a small footbridge extended over the water. On the footbridge, a man stood wearing a uniform with a helmet. The figure appeared to be illuminated. "The photograph was taken by a visitor. What makes it interesting is that we have never had a footbridge extended over any portion of the water. The bridge and person were never there," explained the manager.

He went on to explain that every Halloween the cavern hosts a "haunted cave" ride for the public. One year there were two volunteers who worked at the attraction. "It was their job to conduct a 'fake' séance during one stretch of the ride," said the manager. They did the séance only one weekend. Both men bizarrely died within a week of the séance, on the same day and apart from each other. Did something happen during the séance they conducted that weekend? Did they perhaps make contact with one of the souls who perished in the cave during its construction? Nothing is for certain. Whenever someone begins to explore into the paranormal aspect of the cave, accidents happen. The manager himself ventured into the cave one night with a local ghost hunter only to feel a slight nudge that surprised him. He slipped and broke his ankle. Sometimes if you poke at the paranormal, it pokes back.

OLD FORT NIAGARA

Youngstown, New York
www.OldFortNiagara.com

Paranormal investigators, clergy and scholars are constantly debating why a specific location may become haunted. It has been the experience and belief of the Reverend Tim Shaw that the vibrations of life imprint themselves into the actual fabric of a site. Whether it is because of the geology of the earth's surface, ley lines, aboriginal sources of power or human emotions, it doesn't really matter. What does matter is that there is something that causes this paranormal activity. Over the years that he has been active in the pursuit of the paranormal, Reverend Shaw has found that Fort Niagara is one of those special places.

This location has been busy with human activity since ancient times. Originally, the area served the Neolithic Native Americans as a hunting camp, and later as a base for several post–European contact period explorers, most notably Sieur de La Salle. As a military fortification, the area guarded the entrance to the portage that went around Niagara Falls and, as a result, was the scene of several battles, including the 1759 siege during the French and Indian War and the infamous Iroquois winter of starvation during the Revolutionary. Along with military engagements, the fort witnessed much suffering through disease and malnutrition. It remained in some level of use until 1963, when the federal government decommissioned the site. Today it serves as a historical park and landmark.

Shaw has visited Old Fort Niagara for a good portion of his life. He recalls that some of his best memories are of him and his father playing on the grassy artillery casements and running up the stairs in the redoubts. Over time, he became a costumed volunteer interpreter at the site, portraying the

Fort Niagara. *Photograph by Niagara Falls Paranormal.*

everyday life of a fort artisan. Shortly after his father passed away, Shaw had his first paranormal experience at the fort. He remembers that he visited there for a lecture and decided to walk the grounds for a bit afterward. It was in the early spring and was a bit of a gray day. Since it was early in the season, there were only a handful of tourists there and a skeleton staff busy attending to more important matters than him. As he walked, he felt a draw to what was the old French warehouse that presently is the location of the administration offices and a hall containing a relief map. When he looked, he saw a man walk into the hall who seemed vaguely familiar. Thinking that perhaps he might know this person, he followed him into the building. However, once inside, he realized that he was alone. "Huh," he thought as he looked around. Thinking that he had been mistaken, Shaw turned and noticed that the door hadn't closed behind him. Reaching down to grab the doorknob, he felt something "walk through him." He described it as a feeling "like walking through a cobweb." Before he could reach the handle of the door, it slammed in front of him with a loud bang.

Shaw recalls one evening when he had the opportunity to sleep over at the fort, one of the perks of being a reenactor. He was in the Johnson Room, which is currently set up as a ground-floor dining area. He remembers lying on the wooden floor when he got a chill that he could not shake. He knew that the doors to the structure were bolted and that everyone had gone

Spirits are found with the "spirits" here. *Photograph by Niagara Falls Paranormal.*

home, so he covered himself with his blankets and attempted to get some sleep. As he drifted off, he began to hear voices but didn't think much of it; since there was a Coast Guard base right next door, he assumed that it was just them. But shortly after falling asleep, he awoke to hear what sounded like a door being closed on the second floor above him. He froze, not really knowing or understanding what was going on. Very faintly, he heard what he thought were footsteps echoing from upstairs. They started at the far end of the hallway and started to head for the stairwell. He could hear heels stepping onto the first wooden stair. He ran for the door, flung the bolt open and ran for his car.

Others have experienced the ghostly phenomenon at Old Fort Niagara as well. One story says that during a small reenactor event, two volunteers spotted a woman dressed in white strolling through the fort's burial grounds next to the lighthouse. There have also been reports of a curious group of people, dressed in white, doing what looked like a snake dance. They would first coil themselves and then straighten out. When approached by individuals, the group would vanish.

Old Fort Niagara is now a peaceful place, although the echo of a sometimes cruel and violent past does linger. If you ever have the opportunity to visit the fort, do so when the sun goes down and candlelight casts long shadows upon the gray stone walls; this is when it is at its most beautiful. It is an excellent place for people to experience memories of this world and perhaps another.

USS *THE SULLIVANS*

1 Naval Park CV, Buffalo, New York
www.BuffaloNavalPark.org

In the midst of the horrors of World War II, five brothers from Waterloo, Iowa, decided to join the United States Navy. Aside from two of the brothers who were already enlisted,the remaining three brothers took the oath on the January 3, 1942, with the agreement that they all would serve together. Even

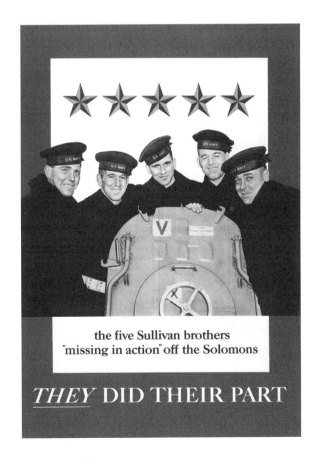

The Sullivan brothers.
Courtesy of the Library of Congress.

though it was policy that siblings did not serve on the same ship, the rule was not strictly enforced. The brothers got their wish and were assigned to duty on the USS *Juneau*.

On November 13, 1942, the brothers were killed in action aboard the USS *Juneau* when the ship sank due to being attacked by a Japanese submarine during the Battle of the Solomon Islands. All five brothers passed away on the same day, on the same ship. There is speculation that some of the crew members on the USS *Juneau* could have been saved, though they were afraid to break the radio silence; therefore, everyone aboard perished to their watery graves.

After the brothers' deaths, the United States Navy decided to name two destroyers after them. These brilliant machines went by the names USS *The Sullivans* (DD-537) and USS *The Sullivans* (DDG-68). After many battles, the USS *The Sullivans* (DD-537) is now at its final resting place in the Buffalo Naval Park. Though the USS *The Sullivans* (DD-537) is a historic landmark, it has had a very eventful life. This ship was the first ship ever commissioned in the navy that honored more then a single person. Built by the Bethlehem Steel Cooperation in San Fransisco, California, at 376 feet and 5 inches long, and with a beam of 39 feet, 5 inches, you can imagine its size when you are standing next to it. It wasn't launched until September 30, 1943. This beautiful naval ship is an example of the Fletcher class. The Fletcher class of ships was the most important in World War II, not to mention the biggest. In World War II, this ship earned nine Battle Stars and two in the Korean War. After the wars, the USS *The Sullivans* was assigned to the Sixth Fleet and was used for a training ship until its decommission on January 7, 1965. In 1977, the USS *The Sullivans* was donated to the Buffalo and Erie County Naval and Military Park.

The Buffalo Naval Park is now used as a historic museum. Anyone can go down on a nice day and tour the beautiful ships as they rock in the water. Aboard the USS *The Sullivans*, there is a memorial dedicated to the boys, and clearly painted throughout the ship are beautiful green four-leaf clovers. This masterpiece is a beautiful dedication to the five Sullivan brothers who lost their lives on that terrible day.

When aboard the USS *The Sullivans*, people have experienced many unexplained and strange encounters. They say that the spirit of George Sullivan still walks the ship dedicated to him and his brothers. They say that he roams the ship in search for the other boys. There have been many claims of moaning and footsteps aboard the ship throughout the night. There was also a story that during an overnight stay on the USS *The Sullivans*, some Girl Scouts woke up to all of the pictures in the museum broken on the floor! It is

Could this be George? *Photograph by Western New York Paranormal Investigation Team.*

also said that when you attempt to photograph the museum of the Sullivan boys, George will not come out in the photo. A more recent story involves an older couple who were touring the ship. They approached an officer on deck of the ship with questions about the Sullivans. He gladly answered the questions the couple had and they continued their tour. As they were preparing to leave the ship, the couple sought the officer out to thank him for his assistance. They were surprised to find that no one had been onboard the ship at that time other than themselves, and there were no naval officers onboard that day.

Inside the USS *The Sullivans* memorial museum there are many photographs and personal possessions on display for the world to see. They are there so that the world never forgets the true contribution and ultimate sacrifice made by the brothers to serve their country. It has also been rumored that their grandmother performed the blessing on this ship. So is the myth true? Is it George walking below the docks looking for his brothers? Is it another soldier who met his demise on the ship, or possibly went back to the ship after his death? No one may ever know the true nature of the haunting of the USS *The Sullivans*, but one thing is for certain: there is a lot of activity aboard!

VAN HORN MANSION

2165 Lockport-Olcott Road, Burt, New York
www.Olcott-Newfane.com/html/van_hornmansion.html

Built in 1823, this mansion was once the home of James Van Horn. Van Horn built the first gristmill in the area in 1811. The mansion is currently owned by the Newfane Historical Society and tours of this beautifully restored landmark are offered daily. As tour guides take visitors through the home, one of the more interesting facts they may share with you is about Malinda, the wife of Van Horn. Malinda died in the home while giving birth to one of their children. As was customary in the late 1800s, many families had family plots near their homes on their property. Her body was laid to rest there, along with the rest of the family members as they passed. In the 1920s, the remains of the Van Horn family were removed from the family plots and laid to rest at a local cemetery, but the remains of Malinda could not be found.

The day the family was removed and Malinda was left behind marked the beginning of the hauntings at the Van Horn Mansion. People have reported seeing a woman standing and looking out one of the upper windows in the master bedroom. When investigated, no one would be in the mansion. Volunteers have heard tappings on the wall, felt cold spots in the building and one volunteer remembers a face-to-face encounter with Malinda when she was wallpapering an upstairs room. As she was working with the wallpaper, she felt the presence of someone standing behind her. She turned and looked to see a woman in period dress standing behind her, just watching. As she stood up to speak to the woman, she vanished.

In 1992, Bruce Ludeman, a special deputy with the Niagara County Sheriff's Department, came to the mansion to assist. Ludeman worked with cadaver retrieval dogs and on several occasions was asked by the Newfane Historical Society to come to the mansion to search for the remains of Malinda. Ludeman recalls spending several nights in the mansion with his wife, a representative of the museum, and one of his dogs, Lobo. Lobo was a yellow lab that was used primarily in narcotics investigations due to his mild manner. Ludeman recalls one night when he came face to face with the spirit of Malinda. He recalls that they were just mingling around upstairs in the master bedroom talking when Lobo began to act restless and began to pace and whimper. His wife was standing just outside the doorway of the bedroom looking over the railing when it all started. He remembers her voice calmly saying, "If you guys want to see Malinda she is standing by the front door." The railing she was looking over had a direct view to the main foyer. Ludeman walked over to the railing and remembers looking down to the foyer to see a hazy mist. It took the shape of a woman that he described as Malinda and then, in a matter of seconds, vanished. This was just one of many encounters that Ludeman had at the mansion.

Later that year, Ludeman was asked to help determine if the body of Malinda did in fact exist on the property. He was assisted by his wife and a close friend who both had excellent abilities with dowsing rods and three of his best cadaver dogs. Ludeman's wife and friend both dowsed the entire property and each determined that the grave, if there was one, was located on the southern portion of the property. When they found the exact location, they drove a steel stake into the ground. It was removed and a second stake was placed in the hole with a sterilized gauze pad on the end of it. The gauze pad was then left on the ground where the hole was dug with the command given to the dogs to find it. At first the dogs seemed to walk around aimlessly, but then one dog picked up on the scent and the others followed.

A few days later, Ludeman returned with the gentleman who runs the local cemetery. They began to dig in the area that the dowsers had discovered and the cadaver dogs had honed in on. After a bit of digging, they discovered human remains. They closed the grave and, with the help of inmates of Niagara County, replaced the grave marker that the Newfane Historical Society had found when it took possession of the house. Since the grave was found and the stone replaced, Malinda has not been seen on the property, according to Bruce Ludeman's 2000 website.

HAUNTED HOMES

Personal stories about haunted locations are often the most accurate. In the Buffalo region, there are some older homes that have great history tied to them, and still lingering inside are spirits of their past. Here are just a few homes with tales of phantom presences.

GARDENIER HOUSE

105 East Main Street, Springville, New York

On any given day, driving down the hill into the town of Springville, your head will turn to see the beautiful homes sitting quietly on their lawns. One house in particular shines out over the others. This Victorian home goes by the name of the Gardenier House. With its shades of blue and gray accenting the beautiful tower off the top of the home, it is a breathtaking site. Built in 1880 by Donald P. Meyers, it was not only an architectural feat but also a beautiful piece of art. The home, even for its size, only took from the summer of 1880 until Thanksgiving of the same year to be completed, for Don P. Meyers was well-to-do and had the money to speed up building. Meyers's story is a mysterious one, all the way from the beginning. When returning to his home of Springville after service in the military, which involved becoming a prisoner of war and surviving, he decided to build this beauty. It was the first private home in the town of Springville to have a telephone. It was also the first residence to have indoor plumbing with a wastewater tube that went out to the neighboring creek. Meyers was a thoughtful man who was also instrumental in building the Civil War statue that sits in the local park today. He would not stay in this home for long, as a week before his birthday, Donald P. Meyers disappeared.

Ghosts of the Queen City

Today, when you want to buy or invest in something, you have many options. Back then, you didn't; you paid with cash. Meyers decided to make a purchase or investment of some sort. To do this, he had to travel from his home toward New York City. He brought $10,000 in cash with him to do so. He was due back that same week for his birthday celebration that was being held in his home on the Fourth of July, but he never returned. Did he take the money and run? Was he robbed and killed? His family will never know.

After he went missing, the house passed through many hands until the present. One woman who stands out in the history of this house is Allison Gardenier, for she was the last person to live solely in this house. After she was gone, the home was transformed into a building with two apartments. Allison, or Allie, as the townspeople called her, was known to be a little different. Bob Simon of Simon Brother's Clothing, a business that was very prominent some years ago in Springville, remembered Allie when he was a child. He told of her playing tetherball in the front yard by herself or always coming outside when the neighborhood kids were around. They always thought of her as a little off, though in my personal opinion, she just sounded lonely.

Theo and Linda Lubke recalled the home before they sold it a few years back. She said that they had never lived in the home but had only used it as a rental. She explained that the house has always been fairly well cared for and that is why the home is so beautiful, inside and out, even to this day.

Its beauty isn't the only thing that makes the Gardenier House so interesting. It also appears to have some paranormal activity in it. There have been many experiences within this home, and they all seem to be relatively similar to one another. The story goes that as you walk by the home, day or night, you can sometimes see a woman standing in the tower looking down, watching out the window. There is also mention of the same spirit lurking in the halls of the home at night. This spirit has been noted to wear a black dress, a white apron and a lace bonnet on her head. A past tenant of the home recalled that when she walked her dog at night, she would often look up into the tower on her way inside and notice a woman standing there. She initially would think that her neighbors had company, but eventually she began to realize that it was happening even when the neighbors were not at home!

Another story goes that one night when a tenant was out of town, she asked her sister to stay at the home and dogsit for her while she was away. The sister awoke in the middle of the night with a chill, and when she reached for another blanket, there was the same woman standing at the end of her bed! Though the spirit was not there to harm her, it scared her enough that she

took the dog in the middle of the night, left the home and never went back
to see her sister while she lived in the house again.

What is uncanny about this female entity whom everyone sees is that she
matches the description of Allie Gardenier! Now, we must ask ourselves,
is this the lonely Allie still watching for children to play with? Is it another
woman, possibly a servant of some sort from the past or a family member
waiting for Don P. Meyers to return home? Next time you are in Springville,
look to the tower and see for yourself.

THE OLD BAKERY

Albion, New York

Old homes hold history and secrets within their walls that many people may
never know. There is a home in the village of Albion, New York, that once
housed a gentleman by the name of Benjamin Franklin. Now this wasn't Ben
Franklin the great statesman and discoverer of electricity. This Benjamin
Franklin was a baker. He operated a small bakery in the village beginning in
1860. It was a small, modest business. He made a good living at it and was
easily able to support his family. He lived behind the bakery with his wife.
Through the years, the bakery was transformed into a primary residence
and, by the 1980s, became several apartments.

One of the apartments became the home of a young couple, Jason and
Lynn, with lofty dreams and goals. He worked in a factory and she was a
cook. They both lived very busy lives and spent very little time in the home
other than eating and sleeping there. There were many times when the two
of them were like ships passing in the night. About six months after moving
into the home, Jason and Lynn were on their way to the grocery store when
another car rear-ended them. It was a very serious accident that left both of
them disabled. At the time of the accident, they did not yet know that Lynn
was pregnant. Fortunately, Lynn was able to carry the child to term and little
Jacob was born.

The road to recovery for the family was a long one. Jason and Lynn both
came to realize that the lives they had dreamed of could not be realized. The
fact that they would both be on permanent disability was difficult for them.
Although they had the joy of watching young Jacob grow, their lives had
changed. It changed in more ways than they would initially realize. As they
began to spend more time within the home, they began to notice things out
of the ordinary. They would hear voices with no explanation. The sound of

a male voice would come from upstairs, there would be children laughing when there was only Jacob and the soft sound of a woman's voice could be heard whispering in the nursery. Late one night when Jason sat at his computer, he saw something fly by the side of his head. If he hadn't known better, he would have thought it to be a small ball of light. Each night it would happen, again and again. He then began to see shadows walking around the home late at night. It made him feel uncomfortable; he began to think that he was just losing his mind, so he chose not to say anything.

Jason stumbled downstairs one morning after what he thought was a restless night to find young Jacob at the table eating his breakfast and Lynn with her hands over her face crying. He asked her what was wrong, and she began to tell Jason of the experiences that she was having in the house. She had woken up about 3:00 a.m. the previous night. She went to roll over but found that she couldn't move; she was paralyzed. She tried to speak but when she opened her mouth, no sound came out. Then she noticed movement out of the corner of her eye. A shadowy figure seemed to walk out from the closet. It approached her and stood over her. It was all black in color and appeared to be wearing a cape of sorts. She finally managed to let out a yell, and as she did, it vanished. Through her terror, Jason did not stir at all. She got up, went downstairs and remained there until Jacob awoke. They now realized that neither of them was alone in the experiences that they were having in the home.

After his bath one night, Lynn took Jacob into the nursery to get him dressed for bed when she realized that she had left the new diapers she had bought in her bedroom. She left the room to get them, and as she did, Jacob began to cry and then to scream. She thought it was just because she left the room for a moment, but it turns out there was something much more supernatural to the behavior. Jason had been downstairs in the kitchen as they were finishing the bath upstairs. He had watched Lynn bring Jacob into his room and then walk back out. They had just installed a new baby monitor in Jacob's room that had a small infrared camera. The camera would allow them to keep a close eye on Jacob at night, especially in light of all the experiences that they had had. As Jason watched the monitor, the screen went from one of peace to one of what could best be described as an orb storm. It began only seconds after Lynn left the room. Hundreds of self-illuminating balls of light began to fly into the room. They came from every direction and speed, changing paths instantly. Jason yelled to Lynn to go back into the room with Jacob. Startled, Lynn hurried back to Jacob, and as she did, the orbs disappeared from the view of the video and the baby calmed immediately. But this was just the beginning for Jacob.

Every night the orb storm would return following Jacob's evening bath. It always occurred when either Jason or Lynn would leave the room. Jacob began to wake in the middle of the night, screaming and crying. By this time, Jacob was eighteen months old and should have been sleeping through the night without a problem. Concerned, one night Jason set up the baby cam in the hallway pointing into the nursery. Like clockwork, Jason woke up in the middle of the night to the sound of Jacob's cry. Lynn went to calm him and Jason went to the baby cam. He had connected a video recorder to it to see if it was one of the orb storms waking him or if it was just Jacob being a toddler. As he watched the video he was amazed and horrified at what he discovered. It wasn't an orb storm that awoke Jacob; it was someone or something in his room. The recording showed a figure appearing to walk slowly out of a wall to the crib, where it stopped for a few seconds before it vanished. Jason walked downstairs to the living room, where his hand-held video recorder was, and grabbed it. With the camcorder in hand, he demanded that what was there needed to leave his family alone and needed to show itself to him. He no sooner got the words out than he felt an unseen force hit him. "It felt like someone punched me in the stomach," Jason recalls.

The family called in a local psychic to help. They had hoped that she may be able to give them a clue as to why there was so much activity in the home, why it seemed to be surrounding their child and why it had become so aggressive with the parents. As the psychic walked through the home, she immediately picked up on Jacob. She told the parents that every person is born with innate psychic abilities but a majority of the people never know about them, and those who do train themselves to use them. Jacob was one of those rare individuals who are born with mediumship abilities. He was able to see and hear the spirits that were around him. He naturally brought them to him because of his unusual ability to communicate. They came to him with the hopes of Jacob sharing their message. Sometimes he laughed and played with them but sometimes they scared him.

She felt that in the home there were two primary spirits that were perhaps once residents of the home. One was a female and the other was a male. As she concentrated on the male entity, the psychic could see a $100 bill in her mind. Jason spoke up and said, "That's interesting because some of the research we did on this home had a prior owner with an interesting name, Benjamin Franklin." The psychic responded quickly, making it clear that it wasn't the same person but just the same name. It was, however, the male entity in the home that was causing the most problems. The spirit still saw the home as his own and couldn't understand why there were strange people living there. Franklin was looking for his beloved wife but couldn't find her.

On the second floor, the psychic felt the presence of a very stern woman. This female entity seemed to feel that she was the caretaker of the child. It was also this spirit that had visited Lynn early that one morning. This woman had died in the home of a heart attack while walking down the spiral stairs.

The psychic explained that the child would have this ability his entire life but would learn to control it. He would be able to filter and change how things appear to him and understand what he sees, hears and feels. Until that time, Jason and Lynn could help. They needed to take control of their home, and the family worked with the psychic to move Franklin and his wife to the light. First they went to Franklin, and the psychic helped Jason to communicate with him. They explained that although this was once his home, it was no longer his. He passed and his wife was indeed waiting for him on the other side. He was welcome to visit the home as long as he did not continue to frighten the family, but for now he had to move on; there were people waiting for him in the light. The psychic went to the child's bedroom with Lynn, where they began to pray. As they prayed, Lynn explained to the female entity that Jacob was her son. She would be the one to take care of him and keep him safe. Her husband was waiting for her and it was time for her to go to him. He had been waiting a long time and she was to go to God. There was a lifting in the air, and the room and home began to feel lighter. The home now had the feeling like after a gentle spring rain.

The home has been quiet since. Certainly Jacob still has his visitations from spirits, but Jason and Lynn now help him to try and understand. They have also come to understand that just because someone can't see something, that doesn't mean they have to fear it. Not everything is bad or evil; it is just not understood.

MAYTHAM MANSION

26 Richmond Avenue, Buffalo, New York

This mansion was built in 1892 by Thomas and Edward Maytham. The Maytham family was known best for the "Tugboat War of the Great Lakes." The family owned an independent tugboat company known as the Maytham Towing and Wrecking Company. The building of the first lock in the St. Mary's River in 1855 provided the opportunity for the transportation of large cargo between Lake Superior and the remaining lower Great Lakes. In order to maximize the profit each company could make, they began to build larger shipping vessels to travel the lakes. In doing this, however, problems began to arise. Towing companies throughout the period from 1855 to 1900 operated with vessels that rapidly became too small to adequately maneuver the large freighters in the Great Lakes harbors. Intense competition for trade placed many of the smaller towing companies in financial jeopardy and the crews in physical danger when inadequately powered steam tugs attempted to tow the growing cargo fleets in the port areas. Damage claims against inept towing services grew, and many commercial fleet owners found their vessels part of a growing backlog of boats awaiting a tug in order to dock. In 1899, these problems forced the Great Lakes Towing Company to be formed, which began to purchase up the smaller tow companies to form a large trust that could handle the shipping dilemma that was beginning to grow. The one company that stood in its way was the Maytham Towing and Wrecking Company.

The Maytham family became well known throughout the country as the one independent company that stood against the trust. In a period of less than six months, the small start-up company went from the operation of three tugs to more than twenty-five, with service from the Atlantic Coast to Duluth, Minnesota, on Lake Superior. It serviced every major port along the trail. Different from traditional tugs, the tugboats of the Maytham Towing and Wrecking Company were made of steel, providing more strength and durability. At the time, each one of them cost $12,000. This was a unique selling point for shipping companies that needed their services, so the company grew quickly, soon having sales agents on the Atlantic coast, according to a 1900 article from the *New York Times*. In the end, it was a short, hot fight between the two companies before the Great Lakes Towing Company purchased the Maytham Company, but it left a mark on American and local history.

The historical district of Buffalo has seen a variety of changes throughout the years. The Maytham Mansion fell on hard economic times and went into a state of disuse and disrepair for some time. It became vacant and a home for vagrants, a "poor women's shelter" and is rumored to have been part of the Underground Railroad for a period of time, according to the *Buffalo Downtowner*'s October 2008 edition. Today, the mansion is the home office for the Buffalo Philharmonic Orchestra, and a bit more. Employees tell of the prankish behavior that seems to have become commonplace at the mansion, from items being rearranged on desks to mysterious electrical problems. One employee shared an experience that she had one day with a little girl at the mansion. She recalled walking up to the main doors one morning to see a woman peering at her through the window in the door. As she reached the door, the woman welcomed her into the building, but when she turned to speak to the woman, she vanished. Others have told of a little girl who plays near the top of the stairs who runs away when approached, disappearing into thin air. Electronic voice phenomenon is also a common occurrence at the mansion. During many board meetings, the directors have used audio recorders to keep records of the meeting, only to go back later to hear the sounds of "other voices" in the room. The unexplained voices are often described as angry or shouting. One has to wonder if these are but memories of the last days of the Maytham Towing and Wrecking Company.

POSSESSED POSSESSION

Nursing Home, East of Buffalo, New York

Western New York Paranormal of Rochester was recently contacted by an adult living facility just outside of Buffalo. The individual who called was the assistant to the executive director of the facility. She explained that over the past six weeks, there had been a large run of bad luck that had occurred at the facility. These events were associated with the property, staff and even some residents. There had also been a history of unexplained activities at the facility in Rochester. In the past, workers had experienced several occurrences in places such as the kitchen, where staff would catch movement of a figure out of the corner of their eye, hear unexplained noises (including a voice saying "hello" when no one else was present) and notice faucets turning on by themselves, among many other unexplained happenings. In the attic area, there could be footsteps heard, doors opening on their own and an overwhelming scent of a rose.

These were all activities that didn't upset anyone; it was pretty much accepted that there was a presence there. In mid-August, things began to change a bit. Chaos began to erupt at the home. Tensions began to rise with unexplained accidents and increased agitation by both staff and residents. Equipment began to break down, residents began to move out and there was an overall sense of chaos. It all began with the appearance of a blessing bowl at the residence. A nurse who worked at the home had taken a recent trip to Africa, where she had come across a very unique gift in one of the public markets: a bowl with hand carvings of an elephant on one side and a rhinoceros on the other. This bowl was traditionally used in religious ceremonies for blessings. She picked up the bowl and returned to the United States with it as a gift for her executive director. Shortly after the arrival of the bowl, their "luck" began to change.

This page: Could spirits be attached to this bowl?

In the last week of September 2008, Western New York Paranormal was called about the bowl and questioned the ability of spirits to be attached to objects. Admittedly, the woman who called questioned if she watched too much *Ghost Hunters* or *Paranormal State*, but I assured her that it was completely possible for "things" to be attached to objects. She went on to explain that they had recently buried the bowl on the property in the hopes of stopping the bad luck, and immediately things began to turn around for them. I explained that there are proper ways of disposing of materials that may have entities attached to them and I would be happy to assist. I also offered to have two psychics look at the bowl to see if there were indeed any residual energies attached.

When I arrived at the home the next morning, workers explained that no sooner had the bowl been dug up than they had to rush a resident to the hospital. Coincidence or not? You decide. I left with the bowl and immediately had the psychic who was with me take it to determine if there was anything attached to it. With the bowl still wrapped in a newspaper so she couldn't see what it was, she immediately began to pick up on sensations of an older black man with salt and pepper hair. She described him as a shaman who used the bowl for magical or mystical practice. She said there was something about his eyes, as if perhaps he was blind.

A few hours later, we met up with lifetime psychic Karyn Reece. Karyn quite often works with Western New York Paranormal on cases, and she took a few moments with the object as well. She described the same man as the first psychic. She went on to say that the bowl was used for blessings and it worked well for people of "white light," while for others it would reflect their energies back to them. So if a person was surrounded with negativity, the bowl would absorb that energy and amplify it. It's not an object that does well around environments where negativity exists.

The object has been placed away so it can cause no influence or harm to anyone. One has to question if this was a matter of perceptions, of people placing blame for normal circumstances on an object, or if it was truly intervention from a far-away land. Regardless, it is interesting how the luck has changed and the psychics both picked up on similar circumstances.

RICHMOND—LOCKWOOD MANSION

844 Delware Avenue, Buffalo, New York

In 1854, Jewett Richmond moved to Buffalo from Syracuse. He relocated to Buffalo and created a partnership that would carry on the grain commission, storage and elevator business. The grain industry was a large economic staple of the region that allowed Richmond to earn a vast fortune rather quickly. In 1871, Richmond purchased a parcel of land on Delaware Avenue, which extended back to what is now known as Richmond Avenue. Sadly, in 1887, Richmond's home burned to the ground. In 1918, Thomas Lockwood purchased the land and remodeled the damaged home. Lockwood was a prominent figure in New York State law, practicing as an attorney and member of the New York State Supreme Court. He remained in the home until his death in 1947. In 1952, the home was renovated and donated to Bishop McMahon High School; it was again renovated in 1969, when it became the Boys' Seminary School. In 1970, IBM attempted to purchase and demolish the building, but it was spared by the Buffalo Historical Society, and now Child and Family Services of Buffalo operates from here.

Haunted houses are often envisioned as creepy, scary places where something tragic has happened. If anything, that image is a stereotype. There is no historical record of anything tragic ever happening on this land or in the building, yet a spirit still wanders the grounds. The spirit is known as "an austere dame, somberly dressed with school marm hair," according to the October 2008 edition of the *Buffalo Downtowner*. Past employees as well as those who work in the building currently know of her presence. Many have said that they can sense a heaviness in the air when she is near. Employees have heard phantom footsteps that suddenly stop, and she is reported to work the intercom system at night, transferring calls. Maintenance workers are also among those who have seen her. They describe her as wearing a floral patterned dress and usually appearing on one of the stairway landings. She isn't transparent, but her colors look faded just before she disappears in front of them.

Once a school marm, always a school marm. Is she a spirit from a school long past coming back to teach lessons to the children?

THE FRENCH WOMAN OF YOUNGSTOWN

Youngstown, New York

Western New York Paranormal was asked to investigate a property just outside of Youngstown, New York. In the home lived a twelve-year-old boy and his two grandparents. The family had always had a great amount of paranormal activity located around the house. The grandmother had conducted some historical research over the years and discovered that the home was resting on what was once a battlefield in the Revolutionary War. In fact, the documents that she discovered stated that the area was also used as a concentration camp for members of the Iroquois Nation during wartime. It's no wonder that there were paranormal occurrences going on around the home.

The grandfather can be best described as a big, burly, teddy bear–type of fellow who always enjoyed watching his wife's interest in the paranormal, although he never put much credence into ghosts. You see, Fred was not much of a believer, or at least didn't let on to that fact. But one night when he was watching television in his bedroom, he saw "something" flash past the window. Not thinking much of it, he ignored it until the next night, when a figure appeared before the window all dressed in white, She was only there for a moment and then was gone as quickly as she had appeared. Since they lived in the middle of nowhere, right on the shore of Lake Erie, he knew that there was no way it could have been a neighbor or a passerby. Over the next few months, the figure would return on occasion to see Fred, perhaps as an admirer.

After the investigation, the team members captured no photograph or video evidence of the woman in white, but they did capture an EVP, a female voice that came out of the darkness to greet the team, saying the word "enchanté," French for "nice to meet you." It seems that Fred has a French admirer watching from outside his window. Why French, you may ask? Their home was located just three miles from Old Fort Niagara, which was originally known as Fort Conti and was built in 1629 as a French outpost. It seems that someone still lingers, perhaps looking for a fallen love who resembles Fred.

THE POLTERGEIST

West Seneca, New York

On a Sunday morning in late summer, Mary was working about her home in West Seneca. Sunday was traditionally the day when she puttered around the house. It was those mornings that always seemed the quietest; there was just a sense of serenity that surrounded them. On this particular morning, Mary was working on catching up on the laundry for the week. She had just placed a load of clothes from the washer into the dryer and turned it on. As she began to walk away, she heard a thumping noise from the dryer. Although she was certain she had checked all of the pockets of the clothes before she washed them, she felt she should recheck them again. One by one, Mary pulled the clothes out from the dryer until she discovered the sound of the thumping. In the bottom of the dryer rested an antique Hesbro self-winding watch.

The watch was one that she hadn't seen before, but she thought that perhaps her husband had purchased it as a gift for himself and just not told her. When Mike came downstairs that morning, she apologized to him for her mistake. She felt that she had washed it by accident, but instead of Mike becoming angry or upset, he acted confused. Mike explained that he didn't have a Hesbro watch. He had no idea where it had come from. Both Mary and Mike were perplexed about the sudden appearance of the watch, but its appearance was the catalyst for what would begin to happen over the next several months in the home and to the family.

Mary had just walked into the house one day after work. Normally, she looked forward to coming home, but as she walked through the door that day she felt uneasy. It was the feeling that a person gets when they're being watched, yet no one was there who could be seen. As she walked into the kitchen, she saw movement out of the corner of her eye. She knew it wasn't the figure of a person, but it was some sort of dark mass that moved quickly and silently. She wanted to look, but the fear she felt made her look away. The thought that was going through her mind was that if she didn't look at it then it wasn't really there. In what seemed like hours, only seconds passed, and she glanced in the direction the movement had come from only to see nothing. Thinking that it was all in her mind, she decided it was best not to mention it to Mike.

The nights in the home began to feel unsettled. Mary and Mike's children begin to wake up screaming. When the parents walked into the children's rooms and asked them what was wrong, the children explained that they were awakened by their beds shaking at night. Their eyes would open to see the shadow of a man standing over them. There were no distinct features to him; he just appeared tall, slender and all black, like a solid shadow. Before their eyes, he would vanish into nothingness. The nights continued to become more active in the household, not only for the children but also for Mary and Mike. Mary began to be awakened at night, discovering burns on her body in the shape of hands, and Mike had finger bruises all along his arms. Every time either of them attempted to confront the spirit that appeared, they would be filled with fear and would feel the need to look down and away. The dogs would cower when the presence came. It was a presence that would move among the shadows and in the darkest corners of the house.

The family had just sat down for dinner one evening when Mike and Mary began to discuss with the children some of the experiences that they had been having in the house. They had hoped that sharing their experiences may ease some of the fear that the children were experiencing. They told of the dark shadows that they too had seen moving about the home and the marks that had appeared on their bodies, as well as the male voice that would appear to be calling their names when no one else was around. They explained to the children that they would make everything okay and they wouldn't be leaving their home. Suddenly, a drinking glass in front of Mike

Spirits at play.

exploded, sending shards of glass over the table. At this point, they decided to call a paranormal investigation organization for help.

Western New York Paranormal of Rochester and Buffalo came one evening in August to conduct its investigation. The organization used a combination of scientific methods and psychic detective work on this particular investigation. The team members stationed infrared video cameras and motion sensors about the home, while individual investigators walked through rooms with cameras and audio recorders. Walking through the home, the psychic investigators felt a very strong male presence. As the lead psychic investigator walked into the laundry room where the watch was found, she picked up the watch and held it in her hand in an effort to gather impressions. Noises began to occur from nowhere. Scratches, thumps and bumps seemed to emanate from all around her. She placed the watch back on the counter and the sounds stopped. She picked it up again and the noises started once more. Taking a moment to center herself spiritually in the room, she sensed the male presence to be a soldier named Anthony William White, a man who never lived in the home. He was from the great state of Kentucky and the watch was once his. In 1953, his fiancée, May Jackson, had given it to him. He prized the watch greatly because it was the last thing she had given him before he left for military boot camp, where he died in a horrible training accident. After his death, the watch was returned to Ms. Jackson until her passing. It then was sold and somehow ended up in the home from one of the prior residents. The psychic investigator sensed that Mary reminded White of his May. He meant no harm but was just trying to get the family to acknowledge his presence.

The investigation continued through the night with camera flashes and audio-recording sessions. At one point, an investigator was sitting in the children's room when a rubber ball bounced into the room from nowhere. A few pictures were taken, but they only showed some potential orb activity. In the end, the team members evaluated all the data collected and discovered that they had indeed captured some unusual phenomena in the home. Mist or ectoplasm was captured in one of the rooms, and there were what appeared to be glowing eyes appearing in the children's room just above their dresser. There was an additional photograph taken from outside the home with the same glowing red eyes captured looking down from the children's window. There were no animals in the home that would account for an eye reflection such as that. There were several EVPs that were captured in the home. Spirit voices reached from the darkness saying, "Hi," "Don't go there" and "Play with me." These sound samples can be heard by visiting the "Buffalo Haunts" section of www.WNYParanormal.com.

The team members suggested to the family that they acknowledge the spirit that was there. They explained that he was there because of the watch and the familiarity that he felt with Mary. They should acknowledge him and explain to him that he was making his presence known in a manner that scared them. If he wished to stay it was all right, but he needed to stop making his presence known in the ways that he had been. Mark and Mary followed the suggestions. Today, the Hesbro watch rests on a special shelf just above the dryer, and the house has been quiet since.

HAUNTED HIGHWAYS

Everyone has heard of the urban legend of the phantom hitchhiker. Every region has a story about a poor soul who passed away on a desolate section of road and has been long forgotten—a soul who appears late on those foggy and misty nights with a warning for those traveling. Buffalo has its share of highway specters as well, some with a friendly message and others…perhaps not so friendly.

THE PIGMAN OF HOLLAND ROAD

Holland Road, Angola, New York

"The Pigman is coming to get you" is just one of the many EVPs that many paranormal groups have captured on a desolate road just outside of Angola, New York. Holland Road has been made famous over the past two hundred years by stories of an entity that travels a small stretch of highway between two railroad bridges. Some have claimed to have feelings of someone watching them from the woods, while others have witnessed white forms moving across the road with sounds of snorts and squeals coming from the darkness.

There are many different variations on the urban legend of the Pigman. Most of them contain an element of truth and a great amount of fancy. In truth, according to local newspaper articles, in the late 1800s a gentleman lived on what is now known as Holland Road. His home was located about halfway between the bridges, set back from the road. Christopher Kester, director of the Chautauqua Alliance for the Paranormal, said that the gentleman was a farmer, and although he did have pigs on his farm, he was not a pig farmer. His name was given to him by the locals due to a facial deformity that he carried. He had a collapsed nose bridge, which caused his

The bridge of Pigman Road.

nose to tip up, much like the snout of a pig. In addition, he also had a cleft palate, which made it difficult to talk. He was a good man who kept mostly to himself, if it was his choice. There were some local teenagers, however, who thought that picking on the "Pigman" was a fun idea.

The teens in the local area would often lure him out of the house with the offer of "smokes." But one day the teasing went too far. A group of three teenagers set fire to his home in three different areas. The building went up quickly, but it wasn't just the home that burned. The Pigman perished inside as he lay asleep.

The spirit of the Pigman
still wanders along Holland
Road, looking for peace.
*Photographs by the Chautauqua
Alliance for the Paranormal.*

Nearly two hundred years later, the legend of the Pigman lives on. Any structure that is attempted to be built between the bridges burns down. According to the local fire department, the fires always start in three places on the property, just as they did so many years ago. There is a stillness that resides between the two bridges like nothing anyone has ever experienced. On a summer day when the birds should be chirping and animals moving among the brush, there is total silence. The local Department of Environmental Conservation doesn't have on record the last time a deer hit even occurred on that stretch of road. Does the wildlife know something that the locals don't?

Many individuals and paranormal organizations have gone to Holland Road over the years in attempts to make contact with the spirit. There have been many reported experiences on the road, including smells of burnt flesh and cigarette smoke, tugs on shirts, sightings of apparitions as well as captured voices and mist photographs. Some have claimed that the Pigman refused to make contact with any mediums that come to the road, but that is not entirely true. In March 2009, Sarah Claud, a medium with Western New York Paranormal, had an opportunity to visit the Pigman. He shared with her that he remains because he just wants his story to be told. He wasn't a bad man, but just misunderstood. People feel his anger when they visit the road because he wants to scare them away. In life, he just wanted to be left alone, as he does now in death.

The Butcher of Angola

Holland Road, Angola, New York

Holland Road is normally associated with the spirit of Pigman, but another spirit resides along the road that many people don't realize exists. He rests just beyond the second railroad bridge, located just a few hundred yards down the road from where his house used to sit. He was known as the butcher of Angola, and in life owned the local meat shop in Angola in the mid-1900s. According to the local legend, he was found hanged on a meat hook in his butcher shop. Today, people see a figure that will hang from the railroad trestle late at night and hear the sounds of heavy footsteps walking down the road. The sounds are like those of a man wearing heavy boots, and some have spotted the apparition of a man in white walking along the road late at night, not seeming to want to hurt anyone.

INTERSTATE 90

Between Buffalo and Rochester

Hauntings are not limited to just objects and homes. They can also occur on the roadways we travel every day. There isn't a city without a tale of a haunted highway traveler looking for a ride or flagging passersby, only to disappear once they have received the attention they sought. Interstate 90, which runs between Rochester and Buffalo, is no different. Jennifer Edmiston recalls one trip she had on that well-traveled highway:

Over the years that I have sensed paranormal presences, the way in which I experience phenomena varies with each encounter. Unlike many that consistently experience with the same set of senses every time, mine truly vary. One of my first naked-eye encounters occurred while driving down a Rochester expressway at about 12:30 at night. I was moving along at a pretty good pace, exceeding the speed limit as I usually do, and as I rounded a bend my headlights shone onto the side of the road, reflecting off the leaves of trees in the distance, and for a brief moment, my lights lit up a man who was standing off the shoulder of the road. He appeared to be standing down the embankment just a bit, and I noted a very clear image of the man: Dark hair, scruffy face and a brown leather jacket. But in that brief moment, I also noticed he had blood on his face and was looking right at me.

Of course, I immediately thought he had been in an accident and needed help, and as I started to put on my brakes to stop and help him, his image quickly disappeared and where I saw the man suddenly a cross with flowers on it appeared. Clearly someone had died in an accident on that spot. You can imagine the shock of first seeing someone injured and in need of help, and a flash of a moment later realizing he wasn't a living person and then seeing a marker memorializing someone's death.

It is my belief that he appeared as a warning that I was going far too fast around a significant bend in the highway. I believe that I saw him that night for a reason, as a sign. I can still see the man's image in my mind quite clearly. It is still my intent to search records to find out the identity of the person who died at that spot, and see if there is any correlation to his image and that of the person who suffered an untimely fate there.

Needless to say, every time I come to that area, I am reminded…and I slow it down.

"SPIRITED" THEATRES

If you want to hear stories about spirits, then dive into the theatre community of any major city. Actors and stagehands have hundreds of experiences that they are always willing to share with theatre-goers. They are a very superstitious folk and go to great lengths to honor the ghosts that inhabit their theatres. A long tradition in theatre is to have a ghost light placed behind or near the stage. There are many different reasons for the ghost light, but most believe that the light is there for the spirits of the theatre. It is believed that actors place so much energy into the characters that they create that they live on long after the performance is through. The ghost light is left on so that the spirits may continue the play long after the living have left the building. Here are just a few of the haunted tales from some of Buffalo's haunted theatres.

LANCASTER OPERA HOUSE

21 Central Avenue, Lancaster, New York
www.Lancopera.org

The Lancaster Opera House claims to be the home of two resident spirits, according to Executive Director Thomas Kazmierczak III. Local legend tells that there were two performers, William and Priscilla, who were romantically involved at the opera house. The couple parted ways romantically when Priscilla moved to Virginia, while William continued to tour with the production company. One day, William decided to visit Priscilla, but before he arrived she was murdered. After William's passing, it was said that the two lovers returned to the place where they were together last, the Lancaster Opera House, according to the 2005 *Amherst Bee*.

Home of the lady in lavender.

Kazmierczak explains that there are numerous stories he has heard throughout his years at the theatre, as well as his own personal experiences. Actors who are performing onstage have shared with him that they have seen a lady watching the performances from the balcony at night. She has affectionately become known as the Lancaster Opera House's "lady in lavender," due to the color of the dress she wears. She is most often seen watching performances that feature actresses in their mid-twenties or younger, for this was Priscilla's age when she reportedly passed away. Priscilla's lover, William, is said to be a friendly spirit full of mischief. He often opens doors, runs the elevators after hours and moves paperwork around. The spirit became such a prankster that actors stopped using the elevator during performances because William would stop it between floors.

The next time you are at the Lancaster Opera House, keep your eyes open to the balcony at stage right. You may just catch a glimpse of the lady in lavender, or if that door mysteriously opens for you and no one is there, it may just be William welcoming you in. It seems that although William and Priscilla are dead, their love for the theatre, and each other, lives on.

RIVIERA THEATRE

67 Webster Street, North Tonawanda, New York
www.RivieraTheatre.org

Built in 1926, the Riviera Theatre was destined to be the "Showplace of the Tonawandas." Its unique architectural style followed that of the Italian Renaissance period, with elegant decor and styling. The crowning pride of the theatre, however, was the Opus 1524 Mighty Wurlitzer Organ. For the first four years, the Wurlitzer was used consistently with performances at the theatre for moving pictures and live performances. As the Depression era struck, the theatre continued in operation under the ownership of Michael Shea. The Riviera became one of the many theatres that he owned and operated throughout the Buffalo region. It remained in the Shea family until the 1960s, when it was purchased by the Dipson Theatre chain. Today, the theatre still remains in operation with live performances and is only one of two theatres in Buffalo to still contain its original organ.

Beyond the history of the theatre, there is a paranormal lore that lives as well. As with many theatres, actors have claimed to see figures sitting in the audience as they practice and perform. Is this a trick of the eye or actually something paranormal? Niagara Falls Paranormal conducted an investigation at the Riviera in the hopes of capturing something. Jimmy Silvaroli, director of the team, shared that the night they visited the theatre, it was pretty uneventful early in the evening. Unlike what most individuals think about paranormal investigation, most of the time investigators are in the dark silence of the location. Rarely does anything go "bump in the night" when they are working on a case. As the night went on though, the atmosphere in the Riviera did begin to change for the investigators. Silvaroli recalls sitting in one of the balcony seats with a fellow investigator when they glanced to their right to see a shadowy figure sitting in a seat a few rows down from them. As they watched, the black, shiny figure stood up, walked away from the seat and vanished once it entered the aisle. Thinking that their eyes may have been playing tricks on them, both investigators went down to the area where they thought the seat was. They sat there for some time, but nothing eventful happened. As they were preparing to move to another location, Silvaroli said that a seat behind him snapped up, as if someone had been sitting there all along. He knows for certain that none of the seats were stuck down but can't explain not only the noise but also the vibration that they felt when the seat snapped. Unfortunately, the only events that were captured on audio or video were the reactions of the investigators, so they don't consider this as proof of the paranormal at the Riviera. But it does add to the question of the phantom audience there.

SHEA'S PERFORMING ARTS CENTER

646 Main Street, Buffalo, New York
www.Sheas.org

Buffalo was in full bloom in the early 1800s. The Erie Canal had just been finished, and Buffalo had become its westernmost port. Commerce was moving into the city, and the population was growing. On April 17, 1859, soon-to-be Buffalo tycoon Michael Shea was born, as shared in the October 2008 edition of the *Buffalo Downtowner*. Shea grew up in Buffalo's First Ward where, at the age of fifteen, he began working. He started out as an ironworker, but later he worked the docks and the freighters of the Buffalo waterfront. But his true passion was for the theatre, where he would find his place in his early thirties.

In 1892, Shea opened a music hall on Clinton Avenue. It became known around the country because of its unique style of entertainment. It remained in operation until a fire in 1904 destroyed the building. This didn't deter Shea, however, because within a year he opened three new theatres in Buffalo: Shea's Travoli on Washington Street, Shea's Court Street Theatre and Shea's Garden Theatre. All catered to the talents of vaudeville. The theatres drew the talents of stars like Will Rogers and Eddie Cantor, and there were rumors that the first striptease was invented by a trapeze artist named Charmion, who removed her jacket and garter, throwing them to the audience below. Shea's talent for the theatre made Buffalo one of the best theatre destinations in the country.

As the years passed, Shea owned a number of other theatres, including one in Toronto. His real dream wasn't realized until January 16, 1926, when he opened Shea's Performing Arts Center. It ushered in a new era of live

Does Michael Shea still watch over his productions?

entertainment for Buffalo. Every kind of showman graced the stage at one point in its twenty-five-year run, including the likes of George Burns, Gracie Allen, Glenn Miller and Tommy Dorsey. Live entertainment wasn't all that saw the stage at Sheas; so did silver screen presentations of Grace Kelly, Charlie Chaplin and many more. Shea worked at the theatre until his death in 1934, but he still remains active in the theatre.

Actors have often looked up during rehearsals to see what they describe as a "distinguished-looking gentleman in a flannel suit" sitting in the balcony. Those who have had the opportunity to have a closer look at him believe that he is the same man whose portrait hangs in the theatre. The portrait is of Michael Shea. A volunteer reported that during the restoration of the theatre, a gentleman approached her dressed in an older-style suit with a white mustache. He looked around and said, "My, how magnificent she is." As the volunteer turned to speak with him, the gentleman vanished.

Those who work at the theatre describe Shea as quite the prankster. Their stories include things like, "I was in the building alone. It was quiet and then the door slammed shut; there was no breeze or any draft. No one else was around," and, "I was in the basement working and felt a warm breath on the back of the neck. I think it was Michael Shea." There have been accounts of Christmas tree lights blinking on and off, which in itself wouldn't be unusual, but they weren't plugged in. Many joke that it was Shea saying "Merry Christmas!"

Sara Hood said it best when she said that Shea put his heart and soul into the building. He's continuing to look out for everything that's there.

STARRY NIGHT THEATRE

170 Schenck Street, North Tonawanda, New York
www.StarryNightTheatre.com

The Starry Night Theatre is a hidden gem in Buffalo's performing arts community. This small theatre is located just outside Buffalo in the suburb of North Tonawanda in what was the first German Methodist church of the area. Still today, if theatre owner Don Swartz were to take you behind the scenes of the main stage, he could show you the original altar for the church, which still exists; the stage was carefully built around it. Construction workers did this as a sign of respect for the place that it once was and the spiritual presence it still brings to the theatre.

Built in 1889, the German Methodist church was to serve the German immigrant population that the Erie Canal had brought to the region. The church was known as the Frieden Church and remained active until June 2000, when it closed. Through the years, the congregation began to slowly splinter off to other churches, leaving an extremely small group of individuals to serve. In 2001, the building was donated to a nonprofit theatre organization known as the Ghostlight Theatre Company, which began, and continues today, renovations of the theatre. Through the years, Swartz has shared that there have been some very interesting experiences that have occurred inside the theatre during performances, practices and even when he has been alone in the building—activities that go far beyond the normal and perhaps into even the supernatural.

One of the most interesting memories was an evening of practice for Charles Dickens's *A Christmas Carol*. During the play practice, Swartz's wife would often take photographs of the performers onstage. One night while snapping photos, she captured a little more than just the two actors onstage. She captured what she believed to be one of the spirits of the Starry Night Theatre. There appears to be the figure of an individual standing behind her husband onstage in the photograph. It could not have been an actor,

A photograph taken during a
rehearsal for *A Christmas Carol*.
Notice the faces of the two spirits
behind the actor portraying Marley.
Photograph by Don Swartz.

The female is believed to be Mrs.
Lavendusky. *Courtesy of Ghostlights
Productions*.

since the space between the actor and the wall amounted to no more than twelve inches. The Swartz family sent the photograph to Western New York Paranormal of Rochester and Buffalo for further examination. What they found astonished the theatre owners. As the photograph was zoomed in closer for clarity, the investigators noticed the images of two spirits. One spirit was that of an older woman in her early seventies and the other was the figure of a young boy with curly hair. Historical records from the church were reviewed, and a photograph that resembled the female spirit was uncovered. It is believed to be one of the founders of the church, Mrs. Lavendusky. This prompted the team from Western New York Paranormal to conduct an investigation of the theatre.

The Swartz family and the actors who worked at the theatre shared a variety of their experiences and stories with the team. There have been instances when a woman in black, who is believed to be Mrs. Lavendusky, can be seen sitting stage right, a few rows back, watching the practice

A haunted bell in the tower?
Photograph by Bruce McCausland.

performances. There have been accounts from patrons who have been at the theatre to watch a performance only to see a figure walk across the stage and then vanish. Everyone has heard noises in the building that can't be explained, such as the sounds of doors closing, whistling and voices calling out. A figure has been seen backstage walking the catwalks late at night, and in the basement the giggles of a little girl can be heard. Swartz jokingly claims that he placed such a heavy door on his office to keep the ghosts away late at night while he's working alone. Actually, he finds that the spirits at the theatre are quite peaceful.

On an investigation at the theatre, members of Western New York Paranormal found just how peaceful the spirits were. Although they captured little in the manner of photography, investigator Jennifer Edmiston discovered that she had contact with one of the spirits of the old church. She was up in the bell tower recording audio when a voice came from the darkness that simply said, "Shhhhh, Vince is coming." A little historical research showed that there was once a gentleman who worked at the church by that name. Could the voice in the tower be that of a spirit trying to hide from Vince, or maybe a bell ringer for the church? Maybe it was one of the last people who rang the bell, for the last time it rang, it cracked the foundation of the building. The bell never rang again.

PARANORMAL TERMS

angel: A benevolent spirit that never lived that watches over and is a servant of God.

anomaly: Anything that is out of place or unexplained. For instance, flare from a camera flash in a mirror is not an anomaly; there is a reason that it happened in the photograph. A mist or vapor that takes on the form of a person is an anomaly.

apparition: This word was used as far back as the seventeenth century in reference to any type of spirit that has the appearance of a solid, physical state.

automatic writing: When a spirit takes over the arm and hand of a medium to communicate through writing down a message using a pen and paper.

black Mass: A satanic ritual performed to mock the Catholic Mass. In the black Mass, the Lord's Prayer is recited backward, communion is desecrated and animals are sacrificed. Other practices include drug-induced sexual orgies in an attempt to acquire more demonic powers.

cleansing: The use of prayer or other ritual to remove negative or unwanted energies from a location.

crisis apparition: Apparitions of the dying or recently dead (usually less than twelve hours, but as much as twenty-four to forty-eight hours after the death) are the most frequently reported apparitions. This category commonly involves one-time visits to someone with whom the apparition has close emotional ties. Though the encounter usually seems to be a type of farewell, sometimes important and useful information is relayed to the "viewer." Though dying is the most common crisis, other life-threatening situations can also trigger apparition visits. In these cases, the crisis apparition typically visits a close associate in an appeal for help.

dead of night: Also known as the "witching hour," this is not midnight. It is actually about 3:00 a.m. This is the time when the veil is thinnest between realms and dark entities are at their strongest power. In many ways, it is a mockery of the trinity and an exact opposite time of when Christ died on the cross.

demon: An evil spirit that never lived, more powerful than man, with unlimited knowledge and power, but still governed by God's rules. In the army of Satan, demons are the grunts of the army.

devils: An evil spirit more powerful than the demon. They have never lived and have no soul. They can be viewed, in a manner of speaking, as the commanding officers.

dowsing: The art of using a pendulum or set of brass or copper rods to communicate with a spirit.

EMF (electromagnetic field): It is believed that all life forms have energy. When they die, the energy has to go someplace, according to the laws of physics; therefore, it is released into the environment. Some believe this to be the soul or consciousness of the individual. Scientific studies have been conducted measuring electrical energy and body mass at the time of death. When death occurs, there is a slight body mass loss and an electrical discharge. It is believed that in order for spirits to manifest, they must gather additional energy, causing changes in the electromagnetic field (magnetic and electrical). These variations can be measured by special meters such as tri-field meters, EMF meters and even compasses.

entity: A ghost.

EVP (electronic voice phenomena): The capture of ghost voices on recorded media. These voices will not be heard at the time of recording but will be heard upon its playback. These are usually simple, one-word responses or short phrases, recorded well above or below the range of human hearing.

Fox sisters: Sisters Kate, Leah and Margaret Fox played an important role in the creation of the Spiritualism religious movement by utilizing spirit communication.

ghost: A spirit that lingers in this world or travels between realms.

ghost hunt: An attempt made by the living to find, see or document a ghost or spirit.

ghost hunter: A living individual who searches out and sometimes finds or identifies ghosts and spirits.

gray lady: The ghost of a woman who has died at the hands of a lover or waits for the return of a loved one.

haunt: A place to which a ghost, or ghosts, frequently return.

haunted: An object, location or person who receives visitations from departed spirits.

haunting: The continuous manifestation of inexplicable phenomena associated with the presence of ghosts or spirits attached to a particular location.

host: Sacramental bread, sometimes called Lamb, which is used in the Christian ritual of the Eucharist.

keening: A loud, high-pitched sound made to mourn the death of a Scottish or Irishman.

ley lines: Energy pathways through the earth that can act as conduits of spiritual energy.

medium: An individual who communicates with spirits.

mist: A vaporous substance that appears in photographs and is believed to be the spirit beginning to manifest.

night shot: Some video and still cameras have the ability to operate with near zero lux, utilizing a special feature that uses infrared lighting.

occult: Studies of the magical or mystical.

orb: A round, white light that commonly appears in photographs in areas that have paranormal activity. Since spherical shapes are the easiest and most coherent shapes to form, it is believed that the spirit orb is the most fundamental of the spirit levels. There is much controversy as to whether orbs actually exist or whether they are simply particles of moisture or dust. Many paranormal groups define true spiritual orbs as those that emit their own light, show evidence of movement and, upon closer examination, have a structural component to them demonstrating a nucleic look inside the orb itself.

Ouija board: A divination tool that allows individuals to speak with spirits. The original Ouija board was simply a wine glass tipped upside down with Scrabble pieces placed on a table. Individuals would touch the rim of the glass and ask questions of the spirits. The glass would then slide from letter to letter, spelling out the response. Parker Brothers later made this game popular, and it is still manufactured in Salem, Massachusetts, today. Many believe that Ouija boards are gateways to the demonic, while others believe it to be the intention placed behind it.

Pagan: A follower of nature-based religion. Pagan comes from the Latin *Paganus*, meaning "country dweller." Pagan is a term used to describe Shamans, Druids, Wiccans, Heathens and other polytheistic religions.

paranormal: Refers to something operating outside the boundaries of explanation.

paranormal investigator: An individual who conducts scientific research of unexplained phenomena.

pendulum: A small weight at the end of a string or chain used for divination.

phantom hitchhiker or traveler: A ghost or spirit that haunts a particular stretch of road or route. Phantom hitchhikers ask for rides only to suddenly disappear when they reach their destination.

photographic apparitions: Ghosts and spirits that you can't see, yet appear in photographs after they are developed.

poltergeist: From the German meaning "noisy ghost," this term has been in use since the early nineteenth century to mean a spirit that makes noise or otherwise plays pranks, often annoying ones. Unlike other ghosts, poltergeists can move from one location to another, following the person they've chosen to torment.

portal: An entry point into our world from that of the spiritual realm. Mirrors are common portal points and have been used for centuries by magicians to scry, or communicate with spirits.

protection: Spiritual ritual, such as prayer, that guards individuals from spiritual attack.

psychic: An individual who receives impressions from the environment and feels energy. They commonly are able to sense energy and its movements.

residual energy: Energy that is left behind after a traumatic or powerful event. This is common in areas such as battlefields, where much tragedy has occurred. Individuals may sense a deep sluggish feeling or, conversely, may feel the powerful positive energy of an excited crowd while in areas such as inside an old theatre.

residual haunting: A haunting that repeats itself over and over again like an old film. Generally, these are caused by a traumatic event.

séance: The gathering of a group of individuals for the purpose of communicating with the ghosts of the dead.

sensitive: Someone who is aware of or can detect paranormal events beyond the range of their five human senses.

spirit: The soul of a human being.

Spiritualism: Formed as a religion in the nineteenth century by the Fox sisters, it is based on the belief system that ghosts and spirits can and do communicate with the living.

supernatural: Something that exists or occurs through some means other than a known force in nature or science.

toning: The practice of using vocalization on specific frequencies to cleanse a home of negative energy.

walkers: Dark, shadowy figures that appear mainly in cemeteries wandering the grounds. They are residual in nature and do not acknowledge an investigator's presence.

white lady: A female ghost who died tragically or suffered greatly in life.

white noise: A sound generated on a single frequency that sounds much like static. It's believed that noise such as this can be used by entities, making it easier for them to produce an audible response.

Wiccan: An individual who follows the religion of Wicca. Wicca is a nature-based religion based on pre-Christian beliefs that honors the earth as sacred and sees deities as both male and female, god and goddess. Wicca was founded by Gerald Gardner in the 1950s.

witching hour: Also known as the "dead of night," this is not midnight. It is actually about 3:00 a.m. This is the time when the veil is thinnest between realms and dark entities are at their strongest power. In many ways, it is a mockery of the trinity and an exact opposite time of when Christ died on the cross.

PARANORMAL RESEARCHERS

Beyond Ghosts Interactive Paranormal: An Internet-based radio broadcast focusing on paranormal phenomenon. www.beyondghosts.com

Buffalo Paranormal Society: A small group based in North Tonawanda, New York. www.myspace.com/buffaloparanormalsociety

Center for Experimental Paranormal Studies: It is their mission to be able to assist both the general public and the paranormal community. This is achieved by offering new methods to better communicate with perceived energy or "spirits," as well as to decisively document instances of paranormal phenomena. CEPS actively participates in a number of ongoing experiments that involve several high-profile locations of paranormal interest that have been well documented by a variety of legitimate sources. www.myspace.com/cepsny

Center for Paranormal Investigation Association: A group based in Orleans County, western New York State. Specializing in investigations pertaining to hauntings and psychic phenomena. www.weirdny.org

Committee for Skeptical Inquiry (CSICOP): A national skeptical research organization based out of Buffalo. www.csicop.com

Lake Erie Area Paranormal Society: A group that investigates paranormal activity, hauntings and any other unexplained phenomenon, provides evidence for the purposes of proving or disproving paranormal activity and provides help and assistance for those affected by whatever may be happening in their vicinity. www.leapsny.com

Niagara Falls Paranormal: A scientific group dedicated to the documentation and exploration of spiritual phenomenon. www.nfparanormal.com

Paranormal and Ghost Society: One of the first paranormal research organizations based in the Buffalo area. Although the group has since relocated to another state, its site still continues to provide a wide selection of information on local haunts. www.paranormalghostsociety.org

Queen City Paranormal Society: This group's goal is to potentially debunk and also disprove claims, with the potential of catching the unexplained. www.queencityparanormal.com

Scientific Paranormal Investigations: This is a group of professionals that seeks out the mysteries of the unknown using logic and reason to prove and/or disprove the existence of the paranormal. www.rochesterspi.com

Western New York Paranormal Investigation Team: A group with the mission of finding and recording paranormal anomalies to prove the existence of the spirit world. www.paranormalinvestigationteam.com

Western New York Paranormal Investigators: A group that operates out of the Buffalo area whose sole goal is to doccument paranormal phenomenon. www.wnypi.com

Western New York Paranormal of Rochester and Buffalo: A group of paranormal investigators in existence since 2004. It is an official 501c(3) nonprofit organization whose dedicated purpose is to help families in the midst of extreme or demonic haunting cases. Members use a combination spiritual and scientific approach to every case with a unique form of grass roots research that helps explain the reason the haunting may be happening. www.wnyparanormal.com

Mason Winfield: A local paranormal author and paranormal historian. www.masonwinfield.com

WNY Ghosthunters: A group established for people interested in the collection of paranormal evidence primarily at historical buildings and landmarks. Members not only love searching for the paranormal, but also the ability to explore unique places filled with years of history. By some accounts of the places they investigate, you could say that they experience "living history"! www.webtvdesign.com

WNY Unexplained Paranormal Society: A group dedicated to exploring the historical and paranormal aspects of suspected haunted locations. www.myspace.com/wnyunexplainedparanormal

BIBLIOGRAPHY

Amadan, April. "Niagara County: Marjim Manor Attracts 'Ghost Hunters.'" *Tonawanda News.* September 24, 2008.

Batterson, David. Personal interview. July 2009.

Beyond Ghosts Paranormal Radio. "Iron Island Interview with Linda Hastriellia." March 4, 2009. beyondghostsip.podomatic.com/entry/2009-03-04T04_38_40-08_00.

Bohn, Marcia. Personal interview. June 2009.

Borick, Anna. "The Haunting of Rolling Hills." *Ghost! Magazine.* 2007. www.ghostmag.com/archive-rolling_hills.htm.

Buffalo and Erie County Naval & Military Park Home Page. "The USS *Sullivans.*" 2009. http://www.buffalonavalpark.org/USSSullivans.html.

Buffalonian. "Buffalo History." 2003. http://www.buffalonian.com/history/index.html.

———. "The H.H. Richardson Complex (Buffalo Psychiatric Center)." 2001. http://www.buffalonian.com/history/articles/1951-now/hhrichardson2002/index.htm.

Business First of Buffalo. "The Ghost of Michael Shea Carries On." August 27, 2001.

Continelli, Louise. "Author Reveals Buffalo's Past." *Buffalo News.* Feburary 4, 2007.

Curtis, Sharlean. Personal interview. July 2009.

Finucane, R.C. *Appearances of the Dead: A Cultural History of Ghosts.* Buffalo, NY: Prometheus Books, 1984.

Gearing, Kathy. The Ghost Club. www.ghostclub.org.uk.

Hill, Barbara. "Historic Lewiston, New York—Devil's Hole Massacre." *Lewiston: A Self-Guided Tour.* 1986. http://www.historiclewiston.org/history.html.

Hirsh, Richard. "$1000 for the Murderer of Christina Jureller." *True Detective.* Circa 1937.

Historic Naval Ships Association. "USS *The Sullivans* (DD-537)." 2007. http://www.hnsa.org/ships/sullivans.htm.

Huson-Krautsak, Libby. "City of Buffalo Cemeteries, Erie County, New York." September 11, 2005. http://wnyroots.tripod.com/index-buffalo.html.

Julio, Dave. "Haunted Places in New York." *The Shadowlands.* http://theshadowlands.net/places/newyork.htm.

Kennard, Jim. Personal interview. June 2009.

Kester, Christopher. Chautaqua Alliance for the Paranormal. Personal interview. April 2009.

Kupczyk, Robert. "Phantoms of the Opera House." *Amherst Bee.* October 25, 2005.

Lockport Cave and Undergrund Boat Ride. www.lockportcave.com.

Lubke, Theo, and Linda Lubke. Personal interview. July 2009.

Ludeman, Bruce. "The Van Horn Mansion." 2000. http://www.angelfire.com/ny4/miaja38/vanhorn.html.

Macken, Lynda Lee. *Empire Ghosts: New York State's Haunted Landmarks.* N.p.: Black Cat Press, 2004.

McQuillen, Paul. "Haunted Buffalo." *Buffalo Downtowner.* October 2008.

New York Times. "Tugboat War on the Lakes." July 28, 1900.

O'Connor, Wendy. Personal interview. July 2009.

Odessa Productions. "The Mystery of Sadie Mcmullen." Online Video. http://www.buffalonian.com/history/articles/1951-now/murder/index.html.

Parkhurst, Frederick, PhD. "City of Tonawanda Cemeteries, Erie County, New York." March 1, 2004. http://wnyroots.tripod.com/index-tonawanda.html.

Powell, Stephen. "The Cholera Epidemic of 1832." *Buffalonian.* 2002. http://www.buffalonian.com/history/articles/1801-50/cholera32.html.

Priebe, Henry J., Jr. "The Village of Buffalo—1801 to 1832." *Buffalonian.* http://www.buffalonian.com/history/articles/1801-50/1801.html.

Real Haunted Houses. "The USS *The Sullivans*." http://www.realhaunts.com/united-states/uss-sullivans/.

Rowe, Rick. "The Forest Lawn Cemetery Investigation." *Paranormal and Ghost Society.* http://www.paranormalghostsociety.org/forestlawn.htm.

Salatin, Steve. Personal interview. July 2009.

Scoville, Dan. Personal interview. June 2009.

Shaw, Tim. Personal interview. September 2006.

Shipwreck World. "Shipwreck Explorers Discover 1780 British Warship in Ontario." June 13, 2008. http://www.shipwreckworld.com/story/shipwreck-explorers-discover-1780-british-warship-in-lake-ontario.aspx.

Sieben, Bob. "The Riviera Theatre and Its Mighty Wurlitzer Piper Organ." http://www.rivieratheatre.org.

Springville Journal. "Whiskey and Cards the Cause of It." June 6, 1906.

Staff of Store Front Education Centers. "Preliminary Report on the Disturbances in Buffalo—June 26–July 1, 1967." *Buffalonian.* http://www.buffalonian.com/history/articles/1951-now/1967riots/index.html.

"The Sullivan Brothers: History of USS *The Sullivans* (DD-537)." *Dictionary of American Naval Fighting Ships.* Vol. 7. Washington, D.C.: Naval Historical Center, 1981. http://www.history.navy.mil/photos/pers-us/uspers-s/sullv-br.htm.

Urlaub, Tricia. "Buffalo, NY Ghosts—Haunted Places in Buffalo." August 13, 2007. http://www.associatedcontent.com/article/340454/buffalo_ny_ghosts_haunted_places_in_pg3.html?cat=54.

USS *The Sullivans* Association. http://www.ussthesullivans.net/.

Vann Ness, Cynthia. Personal interview. June 2009.

Waymarking. "Buffalo, Rochester & Pittsburgh Railroad Station—Springville, New York." October 14, 2007. http://www.waymarking.com/waymarks/WM2D44.

———. "Holiday Inn Grand Island Ghost Story—New York State." November 27, 2007. http://www.waymarking.com/waymarks/WM2NRW.

Wikipedia. "History of Buffalo, New York." June 8, 2009. http://en.wikipedia.org/wiki/History_of_Buffalo,_New_York.

———. "USS *The Sullivans* (DD-537)." http://en.wikipedia.org/wiki/USS_The_Sullivans_(DD-537).

Wilson, Vince. Personal interview. April 2005.

Winfield, Mason. *The Phantom Tour: The 13 Most Haunted Places in WNY.* DVD.

ABOUT THE AUTHORS

Dwayne Claud is an accomplished author and published writer, paranormal investigator, husband and father of three. His other titles include *Baptism by Fire*, *Haunted Finger Lakes: A Ghost Hunter's Guide* and *Rochester Haunts: A Ghost Hunter's Guide*. Known for his passion in the field of investigative research, his experiences span six years and equally as many states. He is the director of Western New York Paranormal as well as a specialist in the field of demonology. He has been consulted by *NBC News Nightline*, appeared on the *Maury Show* and has been a guest on numerous radio shows, such as the *Jeff Rense Radio Program* and *Ghostly Talk*, among others. He enjoys public speaking and can often be found giving lectures on regional hauntings and demonology. His personal interests include hypnosis, hot air ballooning and cooking.

Cassidy O'Connor is a twenty-five-year-old mother of a beautiful three-year-old, a paranormal investigator, a medium and a writer. She focuses much of her energy and writings on the world of the paranormal. She plans on attending school for a master's degree in parapsychology and furthering her career in work with the paranormal. Cassidy is a practicing

Spiritualist and firmly believes in communicating with the dead. Before teaming up with Dwayne Claud and Western New York Paranormal, she accomplished many solo cases. As a solo paranormal investigator, she has opened and successfully closed many cases stretching throughout the area around her. Cassidy has used land association to find many unmarked sites, and has heavily researched a large part of the southern tier of New York State. She is often fighting for historic properties or doing preservation work, and can often be seen photographing historic locations. She is very involved in trying to save local buildings from demolition, as well as working for preservation of local cemeteries. Her hobbies consist of tarot, reading, photography, painting and cartooning.

Other books in the Haunted America series from The History Press include:

  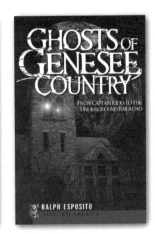

Haunted Rochester: A Supernatural History of the Lower Genesee
Mason Winfield, with John Koerner, Reverend Tim Shaw and Rob Lockhart
978.1.59629.418.9 • 6 x 9 • 128pp • $19.99

Hauntings of the Hudson River Valley: An Investigative Journey
Vincent T. Dacquino
978.1.59629.242.0 • 6 x 9 • 128pp • $19.99

Ghosts of Genesee Country: From Captain Kidd to the Underground Railroad
Ralph Esposito
978.1.59629.811.8 • 6 x 9 • 128pp • $19.99

To purchase, please visit www.historypress.net

HAUNTED AMERICA

Visit us at
www.historypress.net